"Cubs fans, by consensus, are the best in baseball. Year
after year, in good times and (mostly) bad, they turn out in
vociferous numbers, sustaining themselves with a heavenly
ichor that combines loyalty, criticism, cheerfulness,
durability, rage, beer and hope, in exquisite proportions."

– Roger Angell in *Season Ticket*

Published by Wise Guides Inc., Chicago Illinois
Design by IA Collaborative, Chicago Illinois

First U.S. Edition

Wise Guides Inc. is not affiliated with Major League Baseball or any MLB organizations.

2005 Wise Guide™

WRIGLEY FIELD

THE FAN NAVIGATOR TO WRIGLEYVILLE

Table of Contents

Come Across Some Tickets

The most essential part of any trip to Wrigley Field is, of course, the tickets. Because the Cubs have finally figured out how to win and are more popular then ever, it can be quite challenging. If you didn't line up outside Wrigley in the middle of February to buy them when they went on sale, you aren't out of luck. There are still plenty of options to get good seats, from the cheap to the pricey:

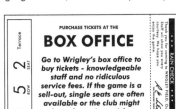

PURCHASE TICKETS AT THE

BOX OFFICE

Go to Wrigley's box office to buy tickets - knowledgeable staff and no ridiculous service fees. If the game is a sell-out, single seats are often available or the club might release last-minute tickets.

SRO
STANDING ROOM ONLY

If you just want in, standing room only tickets go on sale before each game at the box office. There are only about 500 tickets, so get in line early.

LOOK FOR TICKETS ON

EBAY

Many season ticket holders and others use Ebay to dump tickets. Try to sneak in a bid at the last minute and you might get lucky.

22	C	12

51	SATURDAY JULY 30 - 1966 - $2.50

RAIN CHECK
RAIN CHECK SUBJECT TO THE CONDITIONS
SET FORTH ON BACK HEREOF

BUY FROM A

TICKET BROKER

There are several ticket brokers near Wrigley and they're all over the Internet. Be prepared to pay handsomely for seats, but most places are open to negotiation.

$20.00 INCL.10% CITY/COUNTY TAX

Last resort, there are always the scalpers. Check out how to deal with them on page 26.

Mark Your Calendar

Baseball writer Tom Boswell titled his collection of essays on the beauty of a baseball season, "Why Time Begins on Opening Day". Cubs fans may understand the truth in that title better than anyone else. For the folks who made "Wait till next year" famous, Opening Day might just as well be Christmas morning and every other holiday wrapped into one. The calendar says spring but at Wrigley Field Opening Day often dawns with frost on the field, which doesn't stop fans from filling the park and all nearby drinking establishments shortly after breakfast. The 2003 home opener was snowed out and in 2004 temperatures dipped into the 20s. Still, it's a day when all Cubs fans warm to the hope and promise of a new year. Some years, it's the best day of the season.

Things to keep in mind as the Cubs open at Wrigley:

- Cubs have an impressive record in home openers, 75-52-2.

- The ivy's not dead, it's just fallow. It blooms every year, we promise. We make no guarantees about the team.

- Beer stays cold no matter how long you nurse it.

- No need to worry about winter poundage yet … parkas, hats and blankets mask body shape.

Cubs opening day memorable moment:

The Cubs have had some memorable openers, and the one in 1994 was particularly telling: Karl "Tuffy" Rhodes hit three home runs off Dwight Gooden that day and fans at Wrigley thought they'd found the next Willie Mays. They hadn't. The Mets still won the game 12-8 and Tuffy hit only five more home runs all season and finished his major league career with a grand total of 13. He did go on to become a star in Japan, tying the single-season homer record of 55.

Dress Appropriately

Unlike spectators from more moderate climates and those whose teams, against all tradition and basic morality, play indoors, Cubs fans must constantly factor in the weather when planning a day at the park. In fact, there may not be a more challenging setting for the elements in the majors than Wrigley Field.

Opening Day often arrives with temperatures in the 30s, arctic-like wind gusts and wisps of snow. An afternoon game in July or August could mean stifling humidity and temperatures near triple-digits. In May, June or September, depending on where you're sitting and the arc of the sun, you could be sweating and shivering on the same day. It's best to follow the Boy Scout's motto: Be Prepared.

April: dress like you're accompanying Sir Shakleton on his quest for the South Pole: parka, hat, gloves, long underwear.

May/June: most unpredictable time; warm jacket, hat, rain gear, beer glove (one glove to be worn on hand that will hold beer).

July/August: shorts, t-shirts, sun block. A poncho could come in handy when the occasional thunderstorms blow in.

September/October: Not unlike May and June, you just never know. Remember, you can always remove layers.

Recommended wear for women:

April: A, B, E, G, J/L
May/June: B/C, F, I, L
July/August : C, D, F, H, K, L
September/October: B/C, D, H, K, L

Recommended wear for men:

April: G, I, J
May/June: B, C, E, F, H
July/August : A, B, C, D, F, H
September/October: B, C, F, H

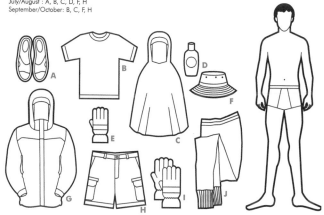

Befriend a Season Ticket Holder

Tickets to Cubs games are as hard to come by as ever, but there is an overlooked potential source of seats: season ticket holders. There are thousands of them out there and chances are you may work with or know one. The wooing of the season ticket holder is a delicate process, though, requiring just the right amount of tact and begging.

How to befriend a season ticket holder:

Start early. Begin courting a season ticket holder as early as a year in advance. Get to know them. Plan social events with them. (ex. Take the ticket holder to Harry Caray's for a steak.)

Compliment them often. On anything. Like their spouse, their kids or their car. (ex. "I hear your Tommy is quite the little southpaw.")

Initiate Cubs talk. Tell an anecdote about the last big game you saw, drop Cubs statistics into the conversation or ramble about your love for hot dogs. (ex. "I have a real hankering for a Hebrew National right now, don't you?")

Seek pity. "I've been dying to get season tickets but I didn't have cash...I lost a bundle in the market...my job was outsourced to India...my wife left me for a Sox fan..."

Become a Bleacher Bum

Wrigley Field's bleachers inspired a long-running stage play, not to mention some of the greatest heckling of all time. Everyone should do it at least once.

Some tips on becoming a bleacher bum:

[1] Get there early: General admission means fans line up a couple hours before the game to snag prime spots. If you're with a group send a couple of people in early to save space.

[2] Scout for seats: If you can't get there early, walk down to the front row and scout for seats from the bottom up. Often you can't see open seats from the concourse. And don't be afraid to ask someone to scoot over a little; they'll be like a long lost friend by the third inning and the second beer.

[3] Bring beers: Speaking of suds, the Cubs bumped beer vendors from the bleachers years ago, so grab one on the concourse on your way in. If the lines are bad upstairs, hike downstairs. You'll be heading down there anyway to hit the bathroom.

[4] Heckle: Give it to opposing outfielders, and expect some to return the favor. Or start up the "left field sucks", "right field sucks" chant.

[5] Woo Woo: Get ready for Ronnie "Woo-Woo" Wickers, who prowls the bleachers almost every game in his Cub uniform. He chants "Cubs-Woo!, Cubs-Woo!, Cubs-Woo!" His stamina will first amaze and then annoy you.

[6] Give back the ball: If you catch a home run ball hit by an opposing player, throw it back or be prepared to feel the wrath of fellow fans.

[7] Grab some ivy: It's possible to reach down and grab some ivy from the top of the wall. Just make sure the security guards are looking the other way. And we didn't tell you.

Bring the Kids Along

There's no better place to spend a sunny summer afternoon with the family than at Wrigley Field. Here are a few tips to make the day memorable and at least a little more affordable.

Come early, leave early. The park opens two hours before game time. It's a great time for the kids to see batting practice and soak up the atmosphere before the crowds arrive. You can get close to the field to see the players and maybe snag an autograph or two. Also, food and non-alcoholic beverages are 25% off the first hour after the gates open. Young children are often pooped by mid-game but that's not such a bad thing; it's much easier getting out of the park and grabbing a cab or the El before the post-game crush.

Bring your own drink and snacks. Juice and goldfish can go a long way, and mixing in your own food with the over-priced hot dog, cracker jacks and cotton candy can save you an extra $20 or so. Also, bring sun screen and baby wipes for the inevitable spills and cotton candy-covered hands and faces.

Buy your souvenirs outside the park. The stands and stores inside the park are busy and usually over-priced. There are plenty of better options outside the stadium.

Make signs, get on TV. WGN loves to show kids and their signs on TV (when the cameramen aren't prowling the bleachers for women in tank-tops). Be creative and don't forget to call grandma.

Stay out of the bleachers. Why expose them to such things at an early age? The bleachers really aren't that bad but there are some fans who see it as nothing less than an open-air kegger. Why take the chance you'll end up next to a reunion of Delta Sigs from State U? Plus, the bathrooms are all the way downstairs and there's nowhere to go if the kids need a break and want to take a walk.

Play a Trivia Game

Wrigley Field has no giant video screen or blaring rock music between innings, so there's plenty of time to talk baseball.

Test your Cubs/Wrigley Field knowledge: draw a line from the question on the left to the correct answer on the right.

1. Last time the Cubs won the World Series	a) 1876
2. Babe Ruth's "called shot" occurred in	b) 1908
3. Bleachers built & ivy planted in	c) 1932
4. White Stockings' (Cubs) first season	d) 1914
5. Wrigley Field was built in	e) 1926
6. Tribune Co. purchased the Cubs in	f) 1937
7. Wrigley Field added lights in	g) 1988
8. Park was re-named Wrigley Field in	h) 1981

Answers:

1. (b) Mordecai "Three Finger" Brown was pitcher.
2. (c) Some say he was gesturing at hecklers in the Cubs' dugout and not predicting a home run.
3. (f) The scoreboard was also constructed during this outfield renovation.
4. (a) The team went through several other nicknames until Cubs was officially adopted in 1907.
5. (d) It's the second-oldest ballpark in the majors to Boston's Fenway Park (1912).
6. (h) The first night game, on 8-8-88, was rained out after 3 1/2 innings.
7. (g) Since then, much construction has occurred in Wrigley Field, including the home clubhouse.
8. (e) In honor of William Wrigley Jr., the gum baron and club owner.

15

Score the Game

Keeping score helps you appreciate the subtleties of baseball and keeps your head in the game. Pick up a scorecard and pencil right inside the gate for a buck or so - it could make a nice keepsake from the day, particularly if something memorable happens on the field. Everybody has their own style for keeping score, but here are the basics.

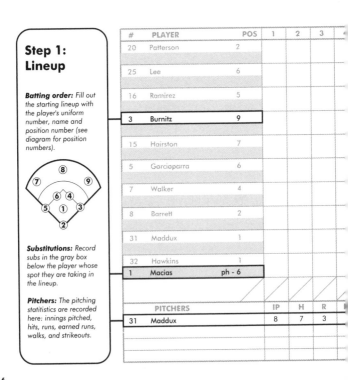

Step 1: Lineup

Batting order: Fill out the starting lineup with the player's uniform number, name and position number (see diagram for position numbers).

Substitutions: Record subs in the gray box below the player whose spot they are taking in the lineup.

Pitchers: The pitching statitistics are recorded here: innings pitched, hits, runs, earned runs, walks, and strikeouts.

#	PLAYER	POS	1	2	3	
20	Patterson	2				
25	Lee	6				
16	Ramirez	5				
3	**Burnitz**	9				
15	Hairston	7				
5	Garciaparra	6				
7	Walker	4				
8	Barrett	2				
31	Maddux	1				
32	Hawkins	1				
1	**Macias**	ph - 6				

	PITCHERS		IP	H	R
31	**Maddux**		8	7	3

Step 2: Plays

Recording Runs: Indicate progression around the bases with a symbol of how the player advanced or the position number of who advanced him. Each corner is a base (first base in the lower right) and move counter clockwise. Circle the symbol in the bottom left to indicate a home run and place dots to show RBIs.

Recording Outs: Indicate the abbreviation and position numbers (See Scoring Abbreviations) of the defensive players involved.

DP	Hit into double
6-4-3	play–short (6) to 2nd (4) to 1st (3)

...he moves to third on Ramirez's (5) sacrifice... ↓

← ...he advances to second due to a walk (BB)... ↑

...and scored on Walker's (4) two run homer...

Patterson in the 1st with a single. (1B)...

5	BB
④	1B

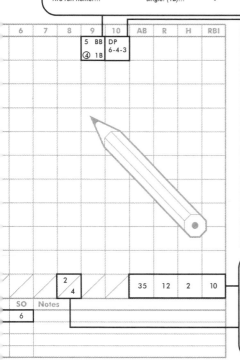

6	7	8	9	10	AB	R	H	RBI
			5 BB ④ 1B	DP 6-4-3				

Scoring Abbreviations

1B	Single
2B	Double
3B	Triple
HR	Home run
E	Error
HBP	Hit by pitch
DP	Double play
SF	Sacrifice fly
SAC	Sacrifice bunt
P	Pop fly
F	Foul fly
U	Unassisted out
BB	Walk
IBB	Intentional walk
CS	Caught stealing
PO	Pickoff
PB	Passed ball
WP	Wild pitch
LO	Line out
FC	Fielder's choice
BD	Balk
K	Strikeout (swing)
⋊	Strikeout (called)

			2 4		35	12	2	10

SO	Notes
6	

Step 3: Tally

Totals: At the end of game total at bats (AB), runs (R), hits (H) and runs batted in (RBI).

Runs and Hits: tallied at the bottom of each inning, number of runs (top) and number of hits (bottom).

Dress Your Dog Properly

**"A hot dog at the ballpark is better than a steak at the Ritz."
– Humphrey Bogart**

At Wrigley, a regular dog costs less than $3 (affordable for ballpark food) and isn't half-bad. Better yet, spend another dollar and get the Kosher dog (bigger, more flavorful and all beef).

As for the traditional Chicago-style hot dog, you can get them at certain stands inside the ballpark but you're better off hitting one of the hot dog places on the outside.

You can't go wrong at Byron's Hot Dog Haus. It's on the edge of Wrigleyville, which, if you want a break from the Mardi Gras atmosphere, could be a good thing. Byron's offers 11 toppings for the complete, singular Chicago hot dog experience.

Just walk three or four blocks north on Sheffield to Irving Park, make a left and you're there (1017 W. Irving Park to be precise). It's just a shack, which somehow makes it all the better.

Use this diagram when dressing your Chicago-style dog:

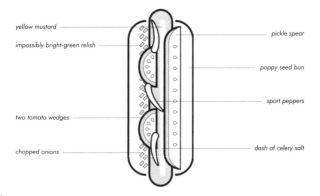

yellow mustard

impossibly bright-green relish

two tomato wedges

chopped onions

pickle spear

poppy seed bun

sport peppers

dash of celery salt

Look To The Flags

A baseball stadium without pennants atop it is like a birthday cake without candles. Seasoned Cubs fans glance at the center field flags even before entering the park to get an idea of what type of game they'll see that day. Wind blowing out: a homer-fest; blowing in: pitchers' duel.

Scoreboard flags: Can't remember if the Giants have overtaken the Dodgers in the West? Below the Stars and Stripes hang the pennants of all the National League teams, arranged by division on three separate poles and in order from top to bottom of that day's standings.

Roof pennants: In honor of former Cub greats, flags mark individual achievements such as Sammy Sosa's 66 home runs, Hack Wilson's 191 RBIs and Greg Maddux's 300 wins, and, well, the team's Pennants.

Foul poles: The three Cubs whose numbers have been retired are honored with flags on the foul polls, Ernie Banks (14) and Ron Santo (10) in left field, and Billy Williams (26) in right. Ryne Sandberg (23) will join them this summer.

Win/Lose: At the game's end, the center-field flags come down and one goes up in their place that lets passersby know the game's outcome. If the Cubs win, a white flag with a blue 'W' flaps breezily; if they lose, a blue flag with a white 'L' hangs its head.

BEHAVE YOURSELF

Wrigley is a place to cheer on the Cubs and have a good time, though there are some rules that make the experience better for everyone. Follow them and you're certain not to alienate the die-hard fans.

1. *SING THE NATIONAL ANTHEM.* Start getting pumped up near the end and cheer the last couple of lines. Think Chicago Stadium, Blackhawks game.

2. *THUNDER STICKS AND OTHER NOISE-MAKERS ARE FOR WIMPS.* If you can't get loud on your own then maybe you're in the wrong place; we hear there are some good chess matches down on the lakefront.

3. *DO NOT DO THE WAVE UNDER ANY CIRCUMSTANCES.* If you see someone trying to start it, firmly tell them to stop, leave the park and go back to St. Louis.

4. *STAND AND SING THE 7TH INNING STRETCH.* The louder the better to drown out the guest conductor.

5. *KEEP CELL PHONE USE TO A MINIMUM.* There's nothing wrong with the occasional call to make fun of a friend who's at work or to let your spouse know you're stuck in traffic. But no one wants to hear your loud descriptions about what you did the night before or why your boss is a jerk and so on. And don't stand up and wave at the camera while talking on the phone.

Dance In The Streets

When summer finally, grudgingly arrives in Chicago, the city comes alive. The lakefront is packed with sunbathers, bikers and boaters, and there's a neighborhood or street festival going on somewhere every weekend. These street fests provide an ideal opportunity to mix with locals, hear some music and sample good food and drink, either before a game or after.

Here are a few:

Northcenter Rib Fest (6/11-12): A mile or so west of the park, it offers great ribs, as well as other foods, beer and music.

Gay Pride Parade (6/26): A few blocks east of Wrigley along Broadway and Halsted, the colorful parade draws hundreds of thousands of people every year.

Chicago Folk & Roots Festival (7/9-10): Good food and great music in the eclectic Lincoln Square neighborhood a couple of miles northwest of Wrigley. Hosted by the excellent Old Town School of Folk Music.

Wrigleyville's Clark-Addison Street Fair (7/9-10): Bored with the view from inside your favorite Wrigleyville bar or restaurant, get up off the stool and head outside. This festival runs along Clark just south of the stadium.

German American Fest (9/9-11): Bratwurst, beer, giant pretzels, men in lederhosen, oompa bands. It's Oktoberfest a little early in what used to be a large German enclave along Lincoln Avenue.

For the larger city-sponsored fests such as Taste of Chicago (6/24-7/4) or the Air & Water Show (8/20-21) see the City of Chicago website.

Buy Something Funky

Retail at Strange Cargo, 3448 N. Clark St. 773-327-8090

Strange Cargo is a hipster's vintage flea market, 3,300 square feet of "That Late-60s to Early-70s Show." Concert T-Shirts, Converse All-Stars, cop shirts and jackets, trading cards, trinkets you might have been playing with 20 or 30 years ago. And remember pea coats? Bell bottoms? Bell-bottomed jumpsuits? It's enough to keep a non-baseball fan coming back to Wrigleyville.

Some of the items you can find at Strange Cargo:

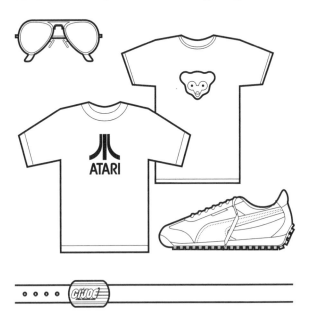

Take a Tour

Wrigley Field is a living museum of sorts, so it's appropriate that the Cubs offer guided tours of the park. There's only so much atmosphere you can soak up in an afternoon at a game; the tours make up the difference. You'll be able to feel the grass of the field under your feet and get a whiff of the Cubs clubhouse. It's a truly inside look at the historic park and worth the price of admission ($20 per person).

The 90-minute tours are held Fridays, Saturdays and one Sunday when the Cubs are on the road, throughout the 2005 season. You'll visit the Cubs and visitors clubhouses, the playing field, skyboxes, the press box, the bleachers and finally end up in the Cubs dugout (spit and scratch away). Cameras are welcome so you can re-live the fantasy later. Get tickets in advance because the tours are very popular and often sell out. If you aren't able to purchase in advance, the Cubs box office releases a limited number on the day of the tour, but they're almost as hot as game tickets.

For further information, call 773-404-CUBS.

2005 Tour Dates

Saturday April 16	Friday June 24	Friday August 19
Saturday April 30	Saturday June 25	Saturday August 20
Sunday May 15	Friday July 8	Friday September 9
Friday June 3	Saturday July 9	Saturday September 10
Saturday June 4	Saturday July 23	Friday September 30
Friday June 17	Friday August 5	Saturday October 1
Saturday June 18	Saturday August 6	

C Cubs / Wrigley Field

Addison
Doors open on the left at Addison;
Welcome to Wrigleyville

RED LINE

Sox/35th
Doors open on the left at Sox/35th;
Welcome to the southside

S Sox / US Cellular

Take the El

The Red Line might be the only thing Sox and Cubs fans have in common. Whether you're heading to Wrigley Field or U.S. Cellular, the El is your best bet for reliable, quick transportation.

The Chicago Transit Authority operates the nation's second largest transit system, and it includes 222 miles of track. The Red Line rides under the city (and under the Chicago River) downtown, and above it north and south. The elevated platform at Addison, rebuilt in 1994 to handle bigger crowds, couldn't be closer to Wrigley ... unless maybe it was in Wrigley. While you're passing through, check out the Cubs-themed paintings featuring greats like Ernie Banks and Ryne Sandburg. The Belmont and Sheridan stops are also within walking distance of the park, as is the Southport stop on the CTA's Brown Line.

It's $1.75, and you can ride as far as you want. On the Red line, that's pretty far. It runs from the city's northern border all the way to 95th Street on Chicago's South Side, where Chicago's other ballpark, U.S. Cellular Field, is located, at the Sox/35th Street station.

Check out www.transitchicago.com for more information.

Prepare Your Speech

Someday, the Academy will award Wrigley Field a Lifetime Achievement Award … or it should anyway. Being the quintessential baseball backdrop, Wrigley has earned cameos and featured spots in blockbusters and bombs, some about baseball, some not.

How much do you know about Wrigley's movie career?
(If you need help, ask surrounding fans.)

[1] In what movie did the cops arrive at Wrigley Field in pursuit of a soul-singing sibling who said his home address was 1060 West Addison?

[2] Which actor and actress caught a Cubs game from a rooftop in "About Last Night"?

[3] Penny Marshall filmed bits of what "skirts in the dirt" movie at Wrigley Field?

WRIGLEY FIELD

[4] Bernie Mac was the star of this movie that was filmed at Wrigley Field.

[5] Who's catch of a foul ball at Wrigley Field was caught on television, almost ruining his cover of playing hooky?

[6] What documentary focuses on the characters of Wrigley Field (the bleacher bums, the ball-hawkers, etc.)?

Probably the best and most poignant film is the documentary about Ron Santo, "This Old Cub." Released last year and directed by Santo's son Jeff, "This Old Cub" looks at Ron Santo's playing career, including the heart-breaking season of '69, as well as his time as a broadcaster and his so-far unsuccessful quest to make the Hall of Fame. It also deals sensitively with his battle with diabetes, which has cost him both legs.

Answers: (1) Blues Brothers (2) Rob Lowe and Demi Moore (3) A League of Their Own (4) Mr. 3000 (5) Ferris Bueller (6) Wrigley Field: Beyond the Ivy

Scalp a Ticket

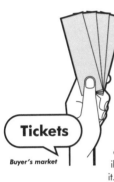

Tickets

Buyer's market

The laws surrounding ticket scalping seem confusing and contradictory, but only if you're paying attention. In Illinois, reselling tickets at more than face value is illegal unless you're a licensed broker. If you operate out of an office, have an 800 number, cash reserves, and register with the Secretary of State for $100, Illinois will license you.

There are plenty of these places around Wrigley (the Cubs set up their own operation to re-sell tickets) and they're all over the Web. Selling tickets on the street for more than face value is, however, illegal, and you can be fined up to $5,000 for doing it. But, and here's the best part, buying scalped tickets is legal.

While scalping isn't for everyone, some see it as a challenge, a chance to test their negotiating skills in the ultimate free market. **Here are a few tips:**

[1] If you want a deal, wait until right before first pitch or until the end of the first inning.

I need four

Seller's market

[2] Disprove the eternal scalper lie: "You're not gonna do any better than that."

[3] Avoid the "professional" scalpers (you'll know them when you see them); instead, find someone headed to the game looking to dump extra seats.

[4] Ask to hold the tickets to check the feel (not laser printed on flimsy paper).

Go to Cubs Jail,
Go Directly to Cubs Jail

Cubs Jail sounds like an existentialist term for what it means to be a Cubs fan. But it's a real place, deep under the stands of Wrigley Field, a place we hope you'll never see. It's reserved for that breed of fan who decides (s)he wants to fight, drink underage, drink to excess, run onto the field or all of the above.

Such a fan will meet an off-duty member of Chicago's finest. Said officer will gladly provide an escort from the sunny confines to the dark, dank Wrigley holding cell. Usually the day doesn't end here; the person will be formally charged and transferred to the Chicago Police station a few blocks away on Addison, where bail and other unpleasantries come in.

Stuff happens when you bring 40,000 people together 81 times during the summer. Happily, most of it's good. When it's not, in addition to security, the Cubs have a medical staff on duty. For minor stuff, you'll always find a nurse located on the concourse behind home plate. The stadium has defibrillators, and the Chicago Fire Department sits right next door (see Thank Your Firemen, pg. 54).

Hit the Road

Wrigley may be heaven but hey, the Cubs can't play all their games there. When the team goes on the road it can be a great excuse to steal away for a little vacation and take in a game.

SBC Park
San Francisco, California

Enjoy the view - you can see both the Giants game and the sparkling bay from a waterfront promenade that borders the outfield.

Coors Field
Denver, Colorado

Catch a Rockies game from the stadium's row of purple seats and you'll be sitting exactly one mile above sea level.

Dodger Stadium
Los Angeles, California

Feel blessed when watching a Dodgers game - Pope John Paul II celebrated Mass here on September 16,1987.

Petco Park
San Diego, California

Appreciate some history at a Padres game. Instead of being knocked down, the historic Western Metal Supply Co. building was incorporated into the park.

Bank One Ballpark
Phoenix, Arizona

Make a splash when you watch the Diamondbacks - the newly remodeled MasterCard Pool Pavilion gives fans an unobstructed view of the action on the field.

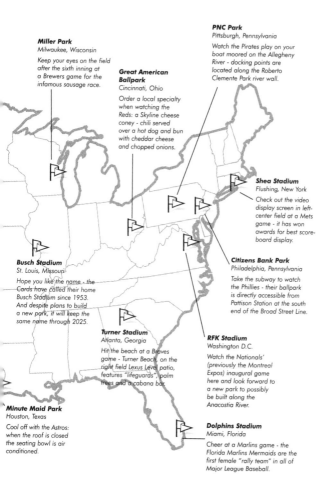

Miller Park
Milwaukee, Wisconsin

Keep your eyes on the field after the sixth inning at a Brewers game for the infamous sausage race.

Great American Ballpark
Cincinnati, Ohio

Order a local specialty when watching the Reds: a Skyline cheese coney - chili served over a hot dog and bun with cheddar cheese and chopped onions.

PNC Park
Pittsburgh, Pennsylvania

Watch the Pirates play on your boat moored on the Allegheny River - docking points are located along the Roberto Clemente Park river wall.

Shea Stadium
Flushing, New York

Check out the video display screen in left-center field at a Mets game - it has won awards for best score-board display.

Busch Stadium
St. Louis, Missouri

Hope you like the name - the Cards have called their home Busch Stadium since 1953. And despite plans to build a new park, it will keep the same name through 2025.

Citizens Bank Park
Philadelphia, Pennsylvania

Take the subway to watch the Phillies - their ballpark is directly accessible from Pattison Station at the south end of the Broad Street Line.

Turner Stadium
Atlanta, Georgia

Hit the beach at a Braves game - Turner Beach, on the right field Lexus Level patio, features "lifeguards", palm trees and a cabana bar.

RFK Stadium
Washington D.C.

Watch the Nationals' (previously the Montreal Expos) inaugural game here and look forward to a new park to possibly be built along the Anacostia River.

Minute Maid Park
Houston, Texas

Cool off with the Astros: when the roof is closed the seating bowl is air conditioned.

Dolphins Stadium
Miami, Florida

Cheer at a Marlins game - the Florida Marlins Mermaids are the first female "rally team" in all of Major League Baseball.

29

Sign Here, Please

Due to the intimate nature of Wrigley, it can be a great place to get autographs. Notwithstanding the somewhat creepy grown men who take this pastime just a little too serious, getting a real live ballplayer to sign your ball, your glove, your whatever, is pretty cool.

Here's how to maximize your odds:

■ Location, Location, Location. If you want it real bad, show up about five hours before game time and wait for the players to arrive. The Cubs parking lot is next to Gate K; the visitors will pull up in cabs at Gate D.

■ Inside before the game, fans are allowed to stand along the low walls in left and right field, just past the dugouts. Usually, a few players sign each day.

■ After the game, head back out to the player's parking lot, where every so often players will sign.

■ Remember your manners. Ask the player politely, don't demand an autograph.

■ Allow kids to go first, don't ask for the player to sign more then one item, and once you get your signature, make way for others.

Use pages 88-91 to collect autographs.

Why Not Us?

The baseball gods really know how to give it to Cubs fans, don't they? Not only did the Red Sox, the Cubs' former compadres in misery, finally win the World Series, but here they come to Wrigley to flaunt it the very next year. Little-remembered fact: Boston's most recent title prior to last year was in 1918 against, you guessed it, the Cubs when a pitcher named Babe Ruth helped lead them to the title.

Cubs fans seem to take one of two attitudes about Boston's title of 2004: it gives them hope because another long-suffering franchise finally won one; or, it annoys them to no end because another long-suffering franchise finally won one.

The visit could provide an opportunity for Chicagoans to pepper Red Sox fans about the miracle last fall:

Q. Has the win changed your life and how?

Q. What did you promise God in return for the title?

Q. Don't the Cardinals suck?

Q. Are you sure that's the same Mark Bellhorn that played here?

Q. Have you ever tried a cup of goat chili?

Speaking of curses, don't let a Boston fan ramble on about breaking the "Curse of the Bambino." Selling the greatest player of all time to your arch-rival is not a curse, it's idiocy. When a Greek immigrant tries to bring a goat to a game, is turned away and in retaliation places a hex on the franchise, that, my strange-talking friend, is a curse.

Put Your Nose In a Book

Wrigley field inspires and sustains people in all walks of life, including writers. Here are a few books that keep Wrigley close to heart.

Wrigley Field: The Unauthorized Biography, by Stuart Shea (2004) – A comprehensive look at the park's history and the characters who filled it, as well as the surrounding neighborhood.

Wrigley Field: A Celebration of the Friendly Confines, by Mark Jacob (2002) – Filled with pictures, this is a great look at Wrigley Field from past to present.

A Day in the Park: In Celebration of Wrigley Field, by William Hartel (1995) Out of Print – On one day, a team of photographers descended on Wrigley Field in order to capture on film what happens from early morning to long after the fans leave the park.

Bleachers: A Summer in Wrigley Field, by Lonnie Wheeler (1988) Out of Print – Although hard to find, this book is the story that captures the heart of the bleachers, and what it's like to go out there day after day.

Murder in Wrigley Field, by Crabbe Evers (a pseudonym for the real authors, William Brashler and Reinder Van Til.) (1991) – A light and entertaining read, this work of fiction begins when the Cubs' star pitcher is shot to death in a tunnel beneath the stadium just before the opening pitch.

Not to be confused with ...

Murder at Wrigley Field, by Troy Soos (1996) – This is a Mickey Rawlings Baseball Mystery.

Cheer In the Bronx

The Yankees are to the Cubs as the Roman Empire is to the Reform Party, Howard Hughes is to Tom Joad, the Rolling Stones are to the Monkees. Whatever the analogy, the records don't lie:

- The Yankees have won 26 World Series, all since 1923; the Cubs two, in 1907 and 1908. Just think, the Cubs would need to win the Series every year through 2029 to eclipse the Yanks.

- League pennants: 39 to 10 (Yankees to Cubs).

- The teams met twice in the Series, in 1932 and 1938, and the Yanks swept both.

- And in the ultimate insult, it was during that 1932 Series at Wrigley when Babe Ruth's "called shot" occurred, the Bambino allegedly pointing to the bleachers and then smacking a home run on the next pitch (the Babe, apparently, could talk some smack).

The historical chasm between these two franchises doesn't mean this series won't be an entertaining one; in fact, it's the contrast that makes it so intriguing. It'll be the Cubs' first visit to Yankee Stadium since the 1938 Series and, if they take one of the games, their first win ever at the legendary park.

If you're planning to make the trip east for the series make reservations early, prepare to spend a small fortune on tickets and accommodations, and bring a thick skin ... New York fans know how to give it. If it gets too bad, feel free to ask them about that embarrassing collapse against the Red Sox last fall or reminisce about the Bulls-Knicks (mis)matches of the 90s. Or better yet, remind them of the glorious June day in 2003 when Kerry Wood out-dueled Roger Clemens at Wrigley in a Cubs win. In fact, the Cubs have won twice as many games as the Yanks in their regular season match-ups. Ok, it's only two games to one, but it's a start.

Don't Be Shy

All that bygone tradition at Wrigley carries a price: bygone facilities. The word "trough" mean anything to you? Going to the bathroom at Wrigley requires forethought.

Some tips for going at Wrigley:

[1] Never *(unless absolutely necessary)* go right after the seventh-inning stretch when every other fan's going to be making a run.

[2] Pay attention to the game and time your breaks appropriately. If there are two outs and the hitter pops one up, start making your way before the ball is even caught. You should be able to make it back before the game resumes.

[3] Upon entering the bathroom, push through the crowd and walk all the way to the back where there's usually plenty of open trough space. This applies for women, too: browse the long line of stall doors, you'll see open ones in the distance.

[4] Do not drink during the game *(can't believe we just wrote that)*.

[5] Scout locations on your way into the park so you're not wandering the concourse aimlessly while the game's going on.

Finally, and this is not a recommendation, there is a device called the Stadium Pal, which includes a bag you strap to your lower leg and that connects to your, ah, well, visit www.stadiumpal.com for more details. Suddenly, Wrigley's troughs seem downright civilized.

Meet Your Neighbors

As a local sports columnist used to write, Chicago is a city of broad shoulders and narrow trophy cases. The Cubs and White Sox have made that phrase a reality with a championship-drought unparalleled in sport: 183 years and counting between them. Still, they've developed a healthy rivalry since the advent of interleague play, bringing an undeniable energy to the park that starts with the fans and translates to the field. Traditionalists argued that interleague play cheapened the game; they probably changed their minds after sitting through a couple of Cubs-Sox games.

The Sox hold a slight series edge, 22-20, and won the only World Series between the two in 1906. That's the year the Cubs set a modern record going 116-36 but then lost to the "hitless wonders" from the South Side four games to two. The heckling and chants go back and forth during these games and fights have been known to erupt in the late innings. But there seems to be a grudging respect between fans; or maybe it's a shared misery. Either way, these games are fun on both sides of town.

Some tips if you're planning to head south for the series:

- Keep it simple, take the red line. The El ride to Sox park is a straight shot south that takes about 30-40 minutes.

- Expect a raucous crowd and don't be afraid to wear your Cubs gear; about half the stadium will be Cubs fans, creating a unique atmosphere where there seem to be two home teams.

- Avoid the upper deck... it really is too high even with recent renovations. The outfield seats are probably the best bargain.

- Chow down; the food's much better and the offerings more varied than at Wrigley.

- Remember: keep your shirt on and stay off the field.

Sing Your Heart Out

Harry Caray, the late, great baseball broadcaster, left behind a tradition that lives on at Wrigley Field: Led from the broadcast booth, everyone rises to sing "Take Me Out to the Ballgame" during the seventh-inning stretch. But most folks (other than south siders) don't realize it didn't start at Wrigley.

Caray first led the stadium chorus unwittingly at the old Comiskey Park while broadcasting for the White Sox. Bill Veeck, who at the time owned the Sox, secretly turned on the booth microphone when he noticed that Caray was singing along with the Comiskey crowd and organist. It caught on, and when Caray left the Sox for the Friendly Confines, he brought it with him. To this day, no matter if the Cubs are trailing by eight runs late in the game, everyone stands and sings.

Memorable recent renditions:

Mike Ditka: A red-faced Mike Ditka arrives just before he's about to go on and screams out the song in about five seconds. He's been back a couple of times to make up for it.

Ozzy Osbourne: Can't blame the England-born rock 'n' roller turned reality TV star for not knowing the words. Even with wife Sharon's help, it was basically unintelligible.

Kid Rock: Kid Rock's posse almost gets into a brawl with sportswriters in the booth next door.

Steve "Mongo" McMichael: After a bad call against the Cubs, the former Bear vowed to have some "speaks" with the umpire before singing. He was promptly ejected from the game.

Bernie Mac: During Game 6 of the 2003 NLCS, Bernie Mac sings "root, root, root for the champs!" rather than "Cubbies." Oops.

Take Me Out to the Ballgame

Vaudeville performer Jack Norworth wrote the song in 15 minutes, according to the Baseball Almanac. The Almanac lists two versions of lyrics: 1908 and 1927. Let's go with 1908—the year the Cubs last won a World Series. Here's the full version:

"Katie Casey was baseball mad.
 Had the fever and had it bad;
 Just to root for the home town crew,
 Ev'ry sou Katie blew.
 On a Saturday, her young beau
 Called to see if she'd like to go,
 To see a show but Miss Kate said,

"No, I'll tell you what you can do."

"Take me out to the ball game,
 Take me out with the crowd.
 Buy me some peanuts and cracker jack,
 I don't care if I never get back,
 Let me root, root, root for the home team,
 If they don't win it's a shame.
 For it's one, two, three strikes, you're out,
 At the old ball game."

"Katie Casey saw all the games,
 Knew the players by their first names;
 Told the umpire he was wrong,
 All along good and strong.
 When the score was just two to two,
 Katie Casey knew what to do,
 Just to cheer up the boys she knew,
 She made the gang sing this song:

"Take me out to the ball game,
 Take me out with the crowd.
 Buy me some peanuts and cracker jack,
 I don't care if I never get back,
 Let me root, root, root for the home team,
 If they don't win it's a shame.
 For it's one, two, three strikes, you're out,
 At the old ball game."

Say Goodbye

Maybe it was simply time for the two sides to part ways. Sammy Sosa was the greatest Cub hitter of all-time and a certain Hall of Famer, but his numbers had slipped in the last few years. There was also the corked bat incident and the walk-out at the end of last year. But there's no denying Sammy WAS the Cubs for 12 years and he will leave a large hole in right field. His trademark sprint to the right field bleachers was a moment of pure joy and brought the bleacher bums to their feet every game. The thought of Sammy doing it in another uniform, for other fans, should sadden even the most cynical Cubs fan.

Top Sammy moments:

- Game-tying two-run homer in Game One of the 2003 NLCS with two outs in the bottom of the ninth. Cubs went on to lose the game in extra innings but that was one clutch blast.

- Twenty home runs is a good year for most major leaguers. Sammy hit that many in one month, setting a record in June 1998.

- Later that summer, Sosa passes Babe Ruth and Roger Maris in dramatic fashion, hitting numbers 61 and 62 at Wrigley in a comeback win over the Brewers.

- In a deeply emotional moment shortly after 9/11, he lofted a small American flag as he sprinted out to right field to start the game. Sosa then homered in his first at-bat and grabbed a small flag from the first base coach and carried it aloft as he circled the bases.

- His monstrous 508th home run that landed somewhere near the Wisconsin state line. The spot on Kenmore Avenue north of Waveland was marked by spray paint.

Good luck Sammy.

Listen Up

When you listen to Ron Santo broadcast a game (WGN AM-720), you feel like you're sitting in the bleachers next to your average Cubs fan. OK, maybe the most passionate Cubs fan on the face of the earth.

Santo's radio commentary can be gut-wrenching. He'll groan when a Cubs fielder boots a grounder and scream when there's a late-inning home run. All the while, Santo's superb broadcast partner Pat Hughes tells you why Ron's so excited. In between, Santo jokes about his own bad toupee or how frugal his partner is.

Since Harry Caray passed to that great sports bar in the sky, Santo has become the Cubs' chief broadcast cheerleader. And why not: Santo played third base at Wrigley for 14 seasons, had his heart break in 1969, and gets as excited as anyone by a nasty Kerry Wood curveball. Santo lost both legs below the knee to diabetes, has a bad heart and faces regular disappointment when the Hall of Fame over-looks him. (He should be in—you can look it up.) But no hardship has diminished his joy for his work or his optimism that the Cubs will win the World Series, with him broadcasting every delicious moment. He is the voice, the heart and soul of the Cubs.

Kill the (Goat) Curse

History points to a goat who knows how to hold a grudge. Pity the poor billy goat. It's hardly at the top of the food chain and is constantly overshadowed by those glamour animals like lions and tigers and gorillas (really, who goes to the zoo to see the goats?) On top of that, Cubs fans have heaped more than a half-century of frustration.

The story, in brief:

William Sianis, a Greek immigrant and owner of the Billy Goat tavern, brought his pet goat to a World Series game at Wrigley in 1945. Sianis had a ticket for the goat but was kicked out anyway. Enraged, he placed a curse on the Cubs that they would never again return to the Fall Classic. Sianis' nephew, who still runs the Billy Goat, brought a goat back to Wrigley to try to break the curse. Still, the World Series drought remains. And skeptical Cubs fans point to the meltdown in the 2003 playoffs as evidence that the Curse of the Goat is alive and well.

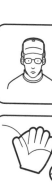

2003: Steve Bartman grabs foul ball, Cubs lose an opportunity for the World Series.

1992: Greg Maddux leaves Cubs after winning the Cy Young award.

1998: Brant Brown drops a ball in the outfield playing the Brewers.

1984: Steve Garvey's 2-run home run in the bottom of the 9th inning gives San Diego a 7–5 win over Chicago.

1969: A black cat runs in front of the Cubs dugout at Shea Stadium.

1989: Les Lancaster forgets the count, gives up game-winning home run against Giants.

Try Something New

Here's a strategy for dispelling the curse of the goat: Eat it. We're not talking goat cheese, though that'd be just fine for an appetizer. Lots of city Mexican restaurants serve goat, especially in tacos. Or if you're thinking about having a goat-themed party, some of the same restaurants will sell you small quantities of goat for your own recipes. Also, try Mexican or Indian markets, and Whole Foods sometimes carries it.

Once you've got your goat, here's a chili recipe:

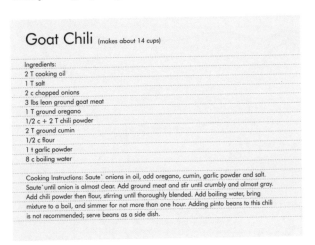

Goat Chili (makes about 14 cups)

Ingredients:
2 T cooking oil
1 T salt
2 c chopped onions
3 lbs lean ground goat meat
1 T ground oregano
1/2 c + 2 T chili powder
2 T ground cumin
1/2 c flour
1 t garlic powder
8 c boiling water

Cooking Instructions: Saute` onions in oil, add oregano, cumin, garlic powder and salt. Saute`until onion is almost clear. Add ground meat and stir until crumbly and almost gray. Add chili powder then flour, stirring until thoroughly blended. Add boiling water, bring mixture to a boil, and simmer for not more than one hour. Adding pinto beans to this chili is not recommended; serve beans as a side dish.

For more information on goats, go to www.greatgoats.com, which promotes goat as "the other red meat."

Use the Seat Improvement Plan

Unless you're stuck behind a pole, and it can happen, there aren't that many bad seats in Wrigley. It's a cozy place where you won't need binoculars to follow the game even if you're in the top of the upper deck.

Still, if you are near the roof or in SRO, it might be time for the SIP (Seat Improvement Plan). Frequently there are opportunities to upgrade your seats during the game. We know some people (ok it's us) that created the following rules for implementing the SIP.

Do your homework: Perched in your 200 level seats, the upper deck or in SRO, keep your eyes open for vacant seats in the 100 level (it is much more difficult to get into box seats). By the third or fourth inning you should have a good idea of who is coming to the game or not.

Send an advance scout: Once your target has been identified, send in a single advance fan to sit in the seats. You'll notice the ushers at Wrigley aren't exactly teenagers on summer jobs. Still, they're spry and you have to be careful. Make your move between innings when there's a lot of traffic.

Blend in: Once your advance person is firmly in place, the rest of the group can join them. Greet each other and others sitting around you, and in general make it seem like you belong. Maybe even pull out a ticket and glance at it like you're trying to find your exact seat. Order a beer and watch the game.

Use technology: If you have friends in better seats stay in contact over the cell and they can let you know if there are open seats near them.

If caught: *Calmly take the "walk of shame" back to your old seats. Protest or in general act like a jerk and you could be headed for a meeting with security. Take your ejection with dignity and the worst thing that can happen is you go back to your original seats and are able to penetrate another breach an inning later.*

Meet Eamus Catuli

Across the street from right field on a building along Sheffield Avenue, and visible to most seats in Wrigley, are two curious signs. One reads "Eamus Catuli". The other lists a line of code "AC 016097" for example.

Eamus didn't play for the 1908 World Champion team and, in fact, never played the game. If you took Latin and stayed awake for class, though, it might make some sense. If not, here's your magic decoder ring, with 2004's numbers:

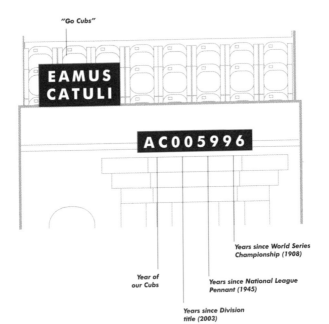

"Go Cubs"

EAMUS CATULI

AC005996

Years since *World Series Championship* (1908)

Year of our Cubs

Years since *National League Pennant* (1945)

Years since *Division title* (2003)

End Up On a Roof

It started innocently enough - apartment dwellers and business owners across the street from the ballpark bringing lawn chairs and a grill to their rooftops to watch the game. Today it's an enormous business. The rooftops are almost an extension of Wrigley with small grandstands and the owners selling tickets and party plans.

After some legal wrangling, the Cubs now get a cut from the rooftop owners in exchange for the team's official seal of approval and a promise not to put up screens that would obstruct the view from the rooftops, as they briefly did a couple of years ago.

If you want to give it a try, here's a list:
Remember, Waveland is beyond left field and Sheffield right field.

Rooftop by the Firehouse
1050 W. Waveland
630-776-4880

Beyond the Ivy
1010 and 1038-48 W. Waveland
847-825-8686 x12

Brixen Ivy
1044 W. Waveland
773-472-7889

Cubby Bear Rooftops
1032 W. Waveland
773-327-1662

Murphy's Rooftop Company
3649 N. Sheffield
773-281-5356

Cubby Bear Rooftops
3643 N. Sheffield
773-327-1662

3639 Rooftop
3639 N. Sheffield
312-382-9100

Rooftop Tickets
3637 N. Sheffield
773-842-5387

Lakeview Baseball Club*
3633 N. Sheffield
773-935-1880

Skybox on Sheffield
3627 N. Sheffield
773-935-3627

Tailgators Rooftop
3621 N. Sheffield
773-477-7725

For more information visit, www.ballparkrooftops.com
* Not endorsed by Cubs

Get Inducted

Ryne Sandberg was a quiet and humble Cub who let his play do the talking in his 15 seasons at Wrigley. He was a slick-fielding second basemen, could hit for average and power, and steal bases. He won nine Gold Gloves, was a 10-time All-Star and retired with more home runs (277) than any second baseman (since surpassed by Jeff Kent).

Cubs fans will always remember him for his play during the electric summer of 1984, when he hit two late-inning home runs in a dramatic win over the rival Cardinals one June afternoon. Ryno went on to win the NL MVP and lead the long-suffering Cubs to an NL East title and the postseason for the first time in almost four decades.

Wrigley, and Wrigleyville for that matter, haven't been the same since. He was elected to the Baseball Hall of Fame earlier this year in his third year on the ballot, which was two years too late for many Cubs fans. The induction ceremony in Cooperstown is the weekend of July 30. Forty-two former Cubs players are now in the Hall.

These inductees spent the bulk of their careers with the Cubs:

Cap Anson	1876-1897
King Kelly	1880-1886
Frank Chance	1898-1912
Johnny Evers	1902-1913
Joe Tinker	1902-1912, 1916
Mordecai Brown	1904-1912, 1916
Gabby Hartnett	1922-1940
Hack Wilson	1926-1931
Billy Herman	1931-1941
Ernie Banks	1953-1971
Billy Williams	1959-1974
Fergie Jenkins	1966-1973, 1982-1983
Ryne Sandberg	1982-1994, 1996-1997

Catch a Ball

Wander out to Waveland Avenue a couple of hours before first pitch, just beyond the left field wall, and you'll see grown men with gloves on waiting for baseballs to drop from the sky. They're the ballhawks who snag batting practice home runs as well as ones hit during the game.

A handful of regulars have been at it for years. Moe Mullins is probably the most well known of the bunch; he's snagged thousands of balls and was all over the news in the summer of 1998 - the year of the great home run race between Sammy Sosa and Mark McGwire - when he pounced upon Sosa's 62nd only to have it ripped from his hands in a mad scrum. He sued the guy who got the ball but dropped the lawsuit when the man agreed to give the ball to Sosa.

If you're looking for some pre-game excitement outside of the local bars, hang out with the ballhawks for a little while. A glove is recommended but not required; the balls often ricochet off the apartment buildings across Waveland and a scramble ensues that requires more agility than equipment.

Keep an eye on the fans standing at the back of the bleachers; their reactions will tell you if one's coming. You'll need some patience, but once you see the ball rocketing over the bleachers and headed your way it'll get your heart racing like you're the Cubs' leftfielder and it's the bottom of the ninth of a tie game.

Jump on a Trampoline

Check out Sluggers, 3540 N. Clark St. Phone is 773-248-0055

Think of it as the mom-and-pop prototype of Dave & Buster's, or of the ESPN Zones now breeding in cities across the land. Or maybe like the old corner hardware store before the day of Home Depot – all the good stuff without the sleek, chain homogenization.

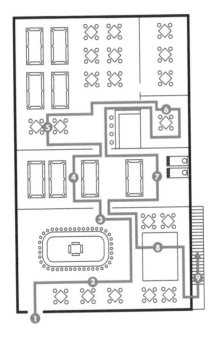

First Floor: (1) Enter. (2) Get a drink. (3) Shoot baskets. (4) Have a private party. (5) Order wings. (6) Play pool. (7) Watch the game on TV. (8) Dance. (9) Head upstairs for games!

Generally, if you like loud, you like a crowd and tons of participatory entertainment, you can't do better than Sluggers. If not, well, maybe you shouldn't be in Wrigleyville in the first place.

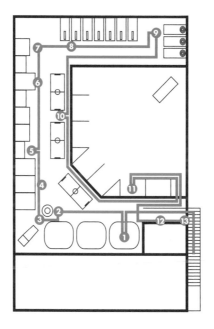

Second Floor: *(1) Jump on trampolines. (2) Spin quarters for prizes. (3) Play Pinball. (4–7) Play video games. (8) Shoot the big mouth gun. (9) Play Skeeball. (10) Play air hockey. (11) Practice your swing. (12) Cash in tickets for prizes. (13) Drinks anyone!*

Check the Score

Nothing - not the Green Monster, not Yankee Stadium, we mean nothing - beats the view of the outfield from inside Wrigley. The red-brick outfield walls are covered with ivy. Above that, a colorful sea of rabid fans in the bleachers. And rising majestically above it all, the wonderful, anachronistic Wrigley centerpiece, the hand-operated scoreboard.

The scoreboard was actually a latecomer to Wrigley. The inimitable Bill Veeck, who also planted the ivy, installed the scoreboard in 1937, along with the current bleachers. The grounds crew operates the scoreboard, some of them veterans of decades.

Check out how quickly the balls and strikes appear after a pitch; the running joke is the umpire waits for the scoreboard to make the call. These eyelets also indicate H or E after somebody bobbles a hot grounder.

You can follow games throughout the league, too, although expansion has meant the scoreboard can't accommodate every team. The operators are pretty vigilant, so if a number hasn't gone up in a while it could mean a big inning for that team. Here's a secret for those out-of-town scores: the number to the left of the team name identifies the pitcher, but it's not his uniform number. It's a number assigned alphabetically, and you need that day's scorecard if you want the list.

	NATIONAL				UMPIRES				AMERICAN				
					PLATE	1ST	2ND	3RD					
	SAN DIEGO				5	22	30	17	NEW YORK				
	LOS ANGELES								BALTIMORE				
	WASHINGTON					**BATTER**				CALIFORNIA				
	PHILADELPHIA									CLEVELAND				
	SAN FRAN					2 2				BOSTON				
	ATLANTA				BALL			STRIKE		SEATTLE				
	PITTSBURGH									KANSAS CITY				
	NEW YORK									MINNESOTA				
	HOUSTON					OUT				DETROIT				
	CINCINNATI									TORONTO				
	ST. LOUIS									CHICAGO				
	CHICAGO				VIS 3	HITS	0	CUBS		OAKLAND				
SP RP	INNING	1 2 3 4 5 6 7 8 9 10							SP RP	INNING	1 2 3 4 5 6 7 8 9 10			

Prepare for the Red Storm

You'll see them strolling Michigan Avenue in their bright red caps, riding the El in packs and, on summer weekends, taking up blocks of seats at Wrigley. They're St. Louis Cardinals fans who make the trek to Chicago every summer to witness a rivalry that dates back to when players traveled by train and these two franchises represented the western edge of the major leagues.

The teams first played in 1892 and have faced each other more than 2,000 times since, with the Cubs holding a slight edge in these match-ups. The Cardinals, though, have a World Series tradition second only to the Yankees, and won the National League pennant in 2004.

All that can make the annual invasion of Cards' fans annoying, but they're almost uniformly friendly, making ballpark trouble rare. (Take a lesson Red Sox and Yankees fans.) Still, a little heckling doesn't hurt.

HEY ST. LOUIS: GET A REAL SKYLINE!

The arch only makes it off the ground by 630 feet while the Sears Tower stands tall at 1,450 feet.

REMEMBER 1984?

Reminisce loudly about when the Cubs beat the Cards in June 1984 and captured the NL East.

BOSTON HAD A GREAT RUN IN '04...WHO WERE THEY PLAYING?

We hope it still hurts that the Red Sox swept last year's series against the Cards.

HOW ABOUT A THANK YOU FOR LOU BROCK?

The Cubs traded him to the Cards in 1964. He then played so well he made it to the Hall of Fame.

LARUSSA LOST HOW MANY SERIES GAMES?... IN A ROW!

In case anyone forgot, that would be eight for the Cards manager.

Drink Beer

"Beer needs baseball, and baseball needs beer - it has always been thus."– Peter Richmond, Author

Beer and baseball go together like, well, baseball and beer. It's hard to imagine one without the other. Vendors at Wrigley mostly sell Budweiser and Old Style. The latter is from Wisconsin but has some-how become Chicago's de facto hometown brew, although some beer snobs turn their nose up at it. For those folks, a wide offering of imports (Heineken, Corona, etc.) can be found at stands on the con-course level. For those with different tastes, frozen drinks and Bob Chinn's Mai Tais are available at certain concessions.

If you don't want to miss any of the game, buy from the vendors - generously tip them and they'll keep finding you. Wrigley Field stops selling alcohol at the end of the 8th inning during day games. At night games, the sale of alcohol stops either at the end of the 7th inning or at 9:20 – whichever comes first.

Use the following map to plan your beverage run:

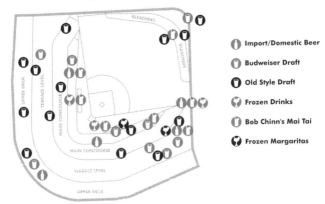

Put Your Name In Lights

Wrigley's made some concessions to modernity, one being the electronic message board that was installed below the otherwise manually operated scoreboard in center field. This addition means you, too, can have your 15 minutes of fame. Well, it might be 15 seconds, but you can get birthday and other greetings up there absolutely free.

Not everything goes, of course. Anything off-color won't be posted. Neither will marriage proposals. Below are some suggestions of messages you might (or might not) post:

To make some new friends:

MEET ME AT MURPHY'S

To lose some friends:

WELCOME CARDS FANS

To ward off another 60-year curse:

GOATS WELCOME

To have your own message displayed: *Write your message to the following address at least two weeks in advance: Scoreboard Operator Wrigley Field 1060 W. Addison St. Chicago, IL 60613*

Thank Your Firemen

Just across Waveland Avenue, in a firehouse built in 1915 expressly to serve the then-newish ballpark, the Chicago Fire Department's Engine Company 78 and Ambulance 6 stand ready.

The firehouse and its fine members have been loyal partners with the Cubs for decades. They've responded to everything from falls to heart attacks. And they don't just help fans. During a Cubs-Yankees match-up in 2003, a big game in terms of history and standings at the time, Cubs first baseman Hee Seop Choi was knocked unconscious after a collision with teammate Kerry Wood. It was a chilling sight made more frightening as Choi lay motionless for some time. Ambulance 6 was there in a heartbeat, driving through the double-doors in right field to transport Choi to a local hospital. (Choi fully recovered.)

Most other interactions have, thankfully, been less dramatic. Former Cubs manager Tom Trebelhorn regularly stopped by for "firehouse chats." Many players do the same over the course of any year. If you get thirsty when you're wandering the neighborhood, the firemen turn a hydrant into a unique drinking fountain. When the dog days turn really hot, they've been known to rig a shower suspended from a street light.

Say thanks: *Wear Engine Company 78's special Wrigley T-shirt. To order one and support the Chicago Fire Department, visit www.chicagofirestore.com.*

Check Out Southport

For those not interested in packing into one of the many bars or restaurants around Wrigley, walk five or six blocks west to Southport Avenue, which has exploded with growth over the past decade. Between Belmont Avenue and Irving Park Road is a corridor full of interesting bars, restaurants and coffee houses, as well as theater and boutique shopping for those so inclined. It's a great getaway from the mobs around Wrigley that's not too far.

Here's a sampling of Southport:

Bars and Pub Food
- Cullens, 3741 N. Southport, 773-975-0600
- Toons, 3857 N. Southport, 773-935-1919
- Hye Bar, 3707 N. Southport, 773-244-4057
- Joy-Blue, 3998 N. Southport, 773-477-3330
- Messner's, 3553 N. Southport, 773-325-0123
- Schoolyard Tavern, 3258 N. Southport, 773-528-8226
- Southport Lanes, 3325 N. Southport, 773-472-6600
- Justins, 3358 N. Southport, 773-929-4844

Restaurants
- Deleece, 4004 N. Southport, 773-325-1710
- Tango Sur, 3763 N. Southport, 773-477-5466
- Red Tomato, 3417 N. Southport, 773-472-5300
- Strega Nona, 3747 N. Southport, 773-244-0990
- Southport Grocery & Café, 3552 N. Southport, 773-665-0100
- D'Agostinos Pizzeria, 1351 W. Addison, 773-477-1821
- Pot Belly Sandwich Works, 3424 N. Southport, 773-289-1807

Theater
- Music Box (movies), 3733 N. Southport, 773-871-6607
- Mercury (stage), 3745 N. Southport, 773-325-1700

Dine Formally

Wrigley will never be confused with one of the shiny new stadiums where you can sit in a glass-enclosed restaurant overlooking the field while you sip a cocktail and munch hors d'oeuvres.

Yet even many Cubs fans would be surprised to learn there are a few places in the park that have actual tables where you can sit and eat, sip a beer, and escape whatever weather mother nature is bringing that day.

Friendly Confines Café: The cafe is located down the right field line, not too far from the Harry Caray statue. What once was a tiny, dingy, restaurant was remodeled prior to the 2003 season, and is one of the nicest stands in the park.

Sheffield Grill: This restaurant and bar is located all the way at the end of the right field concourse, behind Gate D. Since most people stop at the Friendly Confines, this place usually has short lines and plenty of available tables.

Stadium Club: The entrance to this club is located up a set of stairs off of the right field concourse, just before the Friendly Confines Café, but not everyone's welcome. You need to either be a member, which requires season tickets, or be with one.

Upper Deck Patio: While the concessions behind homeplate can get quite busy, an alternative is the patio which was built out over the roof of the park off of the corner of Clark and Addison. The patio has food and drinks and is a great place to take a break and catch some sun. There are terrific views of downtown and the neighborhood, too. There are no TVs, but a radio feed keeps you up to date about what's going on in the game.

Apply More Mustard

You pick up that mouth-watering hot dog and raise it to your mouth, bite down, and suddenly – splat – there's mustard on your pants. Does this common ballpark menace sound familiar? If so, below is an interesting remedy for mustard stain removal.

We learned a lot, maybe a little more than we wanted, about some mustard stain removal techniques from the Argonne National Laboratory's nifty, educational "Ask A Scientist" archives. Here's one:

If the garment is washable, moisten the soiled area with more of the same kind of mustard, allow it to work for a minute or so, and then soak the affected area with a liquid detergent full-strength.

Apparently, the original offending staining substance can contain just the solvents it takes to remove the original stain. Go ahead, give it a try. But be advised: We haven't tried it and accept no liability if you end up with a mustard yellow jumpsuit.

And for more great questions and answers, check out "Ask a Scientist" at www.newton.dep.anl.gov/askasci/gen01/gen01249.htm.

Listen For the Music

Chicago is known for the blues – nothing to do with the Cubs, we swear – but the label's a little misleading because there's so much other great music in the city. There's a thriving alt-rock scene that spawned groups like Wilco and the Smashing Pumpkins (ex-frontman Billy Corgan is a huge Cubs fan), great jazz clubs, reggae bars, a terrific symphony, folk, R&B and even a country place or two.

There are several spots within walking distance of the park where you can sample some of this local sound. The Metro a couple of blocks north on Clark Street hosts alt-rock and punk shows and occasionally draws some big names. If that's not your scene it's still interesting to see the culture clash when a Cub game lets out and tourists in Kerry Wood jerseys walk past a line of spiky-haired teens waiting to get in. A block south of the stadium on Clark are the Wild Hare and Exedus II, cool spots where you can sip Red Stripe or rum and hear some excellent reggae. The Cubby Bear across the street from Wrigley usually has bands on weekend nights, everything from rock to rap. For a more mellow scene and folksy sound, head to the Uncommon Ground Coffeehouse and Café just north of the park on Clark. Many other bars in the area routinely host bands - just follow your ear.

As for the blues, there's no great spot near the park, but two stops south on the red line *(Fullerton Avenue)* are a pair of clubs across the street from each other: B.L.U.E.S. and the famous Kingston Mines, although the latter can be overrun by tourists. A few stops north on the El *(Lawrence Avenue)* is the Green Mill, a classic jazz joint where Al Capone used to go to hear tunes. There are really too many places to name; it's best to pick up a Chicago Reader for a listing of who to see where.

Take Your Vitamins

There's nothing better than a Bloody Mary to kick off game-day in Wrigleyville. A cure for a hangover from the night before or a vitamin-packed breakfast in a glass, the Bloody Mary is one of the few alcoholic beverages that offer nutrition on top of the buzz.

Local Favorites:

Twisted Spoke
Meal in a glass. Thick and spicy.
Served with salami
and cheese.
3369 North Clark Street
773-525-5300

Cubby Bear
Make-your-own-Bloody Bar
Sundays, 10am-2pm.
1059 West Addison Street
773-327-1662

One of our favorites:

Start with 1 full glass of ice

Add:
1 oz vodka
4 dashes Worcestershire sauce
4 dashes Tabasco sauce
2 dashes pickle juice
2 dashes olive juice

Fill glass with tomato juice

Add to taste:
Pepper
Salt

Mix well

Garnish with:
Celery
olives
lime wedge

Watch What You Eat

Tempted to take your shirt off during a steamy day at Wrigley but afraid you'll draw comparisons to ex-Cubs pitcher Rick "The Whale" Reuschel?

If you are on the carb-wary Atkins diet, steer clear of the hot pretzel (79g) or the nachos (50g) and opt for a hot dog sans bun (1g). A friend of low-fat? Order a soft hot pretzel with salt (2 grams of fat) but skip the cheese sauce for dipping (30-70 grams of fat depending on size). A grilled chicken sandwich is better for you than that Hebrew National, but go easy on the condiments. If it's sweets you're craving, try the long, looping licorice, which has only four grams of fat.

Nutrition Facts: Wrigley Field Concessions	Calories	Fat	Carbs
Old Style (12 oz.)	170	0	12
Old Style Light (12 oz.)	113	0	7
Budweiser (12 oz.)	145	0	10.6
Bud Light (12 oz.)	109	0	6.6
Hebrew National	150	14	1
Peanuts (1 oz.)	165	14	6
Licorice	180	4	1
Nachos	500	70	50
Soft pretzel	389	2	79
Popcorn	400	50	16
Pepperoni pizza (one slice)	310	14	33
Sausage pizza (one slice)	300	13	34
Cheese pizza (one slice)	260	10	33

Take a Walk

While the bricks and ivy of Wrigley are charming, there's an architectural wonder just a short walk from the park that's worth a visit – the one block stretch of Alta Vista Terrace.

When work began on Alta Vista in 1900, Wrigley Field didn't yet exist and the Cubs were still playing at the West Side Grounds. Developer Samuel Eberly Gross visited London and wanted to re-create a bit of Mayfair in Chicago. The now landmarked block, also known as the Street of 40 Doors, is a slice of London in Wrigleyville. Pay attention as every charming townhouse on one side is duplicated with only minor variations at the diagonally opposite end of the block.

Location: To get there, walk one block north on Sheffield to Grace and take a left (west). Alta Vista will be on your right; look for the landmark sign.

Tours: The Chicago Architecture Foundation offers a walking tour of the block. The Foundation also offers tours of the historic Graceland Cemetery, just a few blocks further north and the final resting place to Illinois governors and Chicago mayors, business titans such as Marshall Field and heavyweight boxing champion Jack Johnson. The entrance to the cemetery is at the corner of Clark Street and Irving Park Road. You can pick up a map at the office inside the front gate.

Visit their website at www.architecture.org.

Meet Me at Harry

In San Francisco they have a statue of Willie Mays. Outside Busch Stadium in St. Louis there's Stan Musial. Pittsburgh has a trio of former greats: Honus Wagner, Roberto Clemente and Willie Stargell. Guarding the gates at Wrigley Field is no former player, though. The Cubs chose to honor the man that, for better or worse, became the symbol of the franchise in the late 20th century: Harry Caray.

The statue of Caray, who broadcast Cubs games after a long career with the rival Cardinals and a stint with the cross-town White Sox, stands at the corner of Addison and Sheffield, where it's become a shrine. Caray is frozen in a signature moment, leading an imaginary crowd in 'Take Me Out to the Ballgame,' arms outstretched, a microphone in one hand.

The Cubs temporarily erected fencing around the statue after fans began climbing Harry and placing cans of Budweiser in his free hand. Mostly fans just want their picture taken in front of him. It's also a good meeting spot before or after the game, as in "I'll meet you at Harry at 6:55."

Caray has immortal broadcasting company at Wrigley. That "Hey, Hey" you see on each foul pole in big red letters refers to the famous home-run call of Jack Brickhouse. Before Harry, Brickhouse broadcast Cubs games for four decades.

Get a Tattoo

As the crowd disperses after a game, some fans make their way to Clark Street bars, others head to their cars, while some might find themselves on Belmont Avenue, about four blocks south of Wrigley Field.

Here you will see fewer Cubs fans, but no lack of interesting people and places. Though you could grab a bite at Bittersweet, a pastry shop and gourmet cafe, or browse the selection of clothing boutiques, you'll also notice an eclectic mix of businesses such as Egor's Dungeon (a sex shop) and The Chicago Tattooing and Piercing Co., Inc.

More than 25 years old, The Chicago Tattooing and Piercing Company has become a Chicago institution for safe, quality and artistic tattoos. Open seven days a week, noon until midnight, it might make for an intriguing stop pre or post game. Tattoo price depends upon size, placement and detail, and starts at $50. Choose from one of their many designs displayed on their walls or bring in your own artwork - a large red "C" perhaps? With a blue circle around it? We'll leave that to your discretion.

Chicago Tattoo
922 W. Belmont
773-528-6969

Imagine da Bears Here

The gridiron ran north-south, with the end zones buffeted by the visitors' dugout and the left field wall.

Wrigley Field has hosted some electrifying performances over the years, maybe none more so than on Dec.12, 1965. No, the Cubs weren't deep into the playoffs then.

The Bears still played in Wrigley, and rookie Gayle Sayers ran for six touchdowns that day on a muddy field that made everyone else look like they were playing in slow motion.

It's fun to sit back on a warm summer day at Wrigley and try to picture Sayers or "Red Grange" darting away from defenders, Dick Butkus putting a punishing hit on an opposing ball carrier or 'Papa Bear' Halas prowling the sidelines.

Some trivia sure to win you an Old Style:

- The Bears called Wrigley Field home from 1921-1970.

- The Bears played 332 games at Wrigley (221-89-22), the most ever played by one team in a home stadium in NFL history.

- They won four NFL Championships at Wrigley, the last a 14-10 win over the New York Giants in 1963.

Cubstock or Bust

For Cubs fans, it usually starts the first week of October: the dreaded
BDS (baseball deprivation syndrome). It gets worse as winter sets
in. Come January, though, relief arrives in the form of the Cubs
Convention. The convention has been held for the past 20 years,
usually in late January, and is a weekend-long celebration of all
things Cub. Meet Cubs players past and present, get autographs,
hear from the manager and team execs, buy Cubs paraphernalia.

The convention sells out every year but one way to ensure a ticket is
to book a room at the host site, the Chicago Hilton and Towers, when
dates are announced (usually around June). Your room reservation
guarantees up to four discounted Cubs Convention passes. The alternative is to simply buy a weekend pass when they go on sale in
November. But be ready to buy the day they go on sale - in 2004
they sold out in about two hours. If that doesn't work, tickets can be
found online from some of the same folks who sell game seats.

The crowds can be overwhelming and the lines long to meet the
players. But, hey, it's for a good cause. All proceeds from the Cubs
Convention benefit Cubs Care, the team's charitable arm.

Restaurant and Bar (Wise) Guide
Your go-to guide for Wrigleyville

Bacci Pizzeria

950 W. Addison St.
773-305-4100

Conveniently located right next to the El stop, this family-run pizza chain offers a jumbo slice and free pop for $3.50, which is definitely enough to fill you up.

Bar Celona and Grill

3474 N. Clark St.
773-244-8000

Smaller restaurant seating 80 people with Spanish and Mexican tapas-style cuisine. The garage door front opens so you can feel part of the street action.

Bar Louie

3545 N. Clark St.
773-296-2500

Creative martinis top the drink menu. Expect a big crowd. Bar Louie is a chain, but each one fits its neighborhood nicely. The oversized mural of Wrigley Field from the bleachers makes you feel like you're still in the stadium.

Bernie's

3664 N. Clark St.
773-525-1898.

Outdoor beer garden. The see and be seen place where hard core fans and occasionally players hang out before and after the game (the players only after).

Blarney Stone

3424 N. Sheffield Ave.
773-348-1078

A classic neighborhood spot – smoky with the wear of a 35-year-old bar. Cocktails flow generously.

Casey Moran's

3660 N. Clark St.
773-755-4444

Opened in 2004, Metromix uses words like elegant and classy to describe this place right across the street from Wrigley. Considering its location they're not far off. Lots of plasma screens, two bars and bar food.

Chen's Chinese

3510 N. Clark St.

773-549-1280

Billed as "Chinese, Sushi and Saki" Lounge. Pan-Asian specialties in a quiet room lined with fish tanks.

Cubby Bear Lounge

1059 W. Addison St.

773-327-1662

Packed before and after games, it's a huge place so it can handle the crowds. Vies with Murphy's as the pre/post game destination of the masses. Being part of the masses is fun, sometimes.

The Dark Horse Tap and Grille

3443 N. Sheffield Ave.

773-248-4400

Three-dollar hot dogs smothered in chili, onions and cheese are worth making the Dark Horse a stop. Dark Horse tries to walk the line between loud sports bar (TVs galore) and trendy lounge (mahogany walls). You be the judge if it works.

El Jardin Café

3401 N. Clark St.

773-935-8133

El Jardin Restaurant

3335 N. Clark St.

773-528-6775

Every Northsider has a story of debauchery that begins with, "I had a couple margaritas at El Jardin's and…". Food is good, lines are way long and did we mention that night we had a couple margaritas at El Jardin…

Exedus II

3477 N. Clark St.

773-348-3998

Loud and live. Excellent reggae music seven nights a week and expect an interesting crowd.

Fly Me to the Moon

3400 N. Clark St.

773-528-4033

Restaurant with piano music and live vocalists most nights, and after 10, tables are rolled back for dancing. Menu is an eclectic mix of Italian and Greek specialties.

The Full Shilling Public House
3724 N. Clark St.
773-248-3330

A lot of Cubs fans died a little when the Wrigleyville Tap closed, but this place has grown on us. They serve all the food you would expect, and it's a popular spot for the regular season-ticket holders to gather after Cubs games.

Gingerman Tavern
3740 N. Clark St.
773-549-2050

Great list of beers, both tap and bottle, and interesting juke box. Drink and shoot some pool in the back, or just chill with the eclectic crowd. This is far from your typical sports bar, although Cubs fans are welcome.

Goose Island
3535 N. Clark St.
773-832-9040

A full micro brewery – always something new to try. They make Chicago's true hometown brew (with apologies to Old Style) and good basic food.

Guthries
1300 W. Addison St.
773-477-2900

Real neighborhood bar a couple blocks west of the park. Fills up after games. They have a cupboard full of board games if you're in the mood.

Heaven on Seven
3478 N. Clark St.
773-477-7818

Outpost of the Loop original with great Cajun. Not-to-be-missed jambalaya or try to tackle a pile of crawfish.

Hi-Tops
3551 N. Sheffield Ave.
773-348-0009

Girls-dancing-on-tables type of place with sixty-five TVs that assure you won't miss one play of any sporting event anywhere. In the shadow of Wrigley Field this two-story bar will quench your thirst and provide you with some quick eats. Packed before and after games.

The Irish Oak
3511 N. Clark St.
773-935-6669

Irish food and drink – from Guiness to Shepherds Pie to the Irish breakfast "fry" that's served all day and sure to help you overcome a hangover.

John Barleycorn
3524 N. Clark St.
773-549-6000

Another outpost of an original (in Lincoln Park) with good, inexpensive eats and lots of drink in this huge two-story bar.

Johnny O'Hagan's
3374 N. Clark St.
773-248-3600

Did we say Irish? The bar immigrated from the Emerald Isle and everything, from the fish-and-chips to the fireplaces, matches.

Lucky's Sandwich Company
3472 N. Clark St.
773-549-0665

In a concept borrowed from Pittsburgh, this sandwich shop features "overstuffed" sandwiches, where the fries are layered on top of the meat. BYOB.

Merkle's Bar & Grill
3516 N. Clark St.
773-244-1025

A brand new addition to Wrigleyville, this bar serves all the classic American food and also features a bunch of plasmas making it a great place to catch a game.

Matsuya
3469 N. Clark St.
773-248-2677

Always packed – and deservedly so; fresh Japanese food with beautifully presented plates and reasonable prices. Two entrances – check out the line at each to see where you might have the advantage if you're in a hurry.

Metro
3730 N. Clark St.
773-549-0203

This one-time theater has been at the hub of the Chicago music scene forever. Check out the Reader (www.chicagoreader.com) to see what's playing at the Metro after the game.

Moxie

3517 N. Clark St.
773-935-6694

Classy and upscale – hints of a downtown trendy restaurant – featuring tapas and martinis. There's often live music in this oasis from sports.

Mullen's on Clark

3527 N. Clark St.
773-325-2319

Get some local flavor by mingling with the regulars at Mullens – including its softball team, darts league and soccer club. Named after a police officer wounded in the line of duty (see www.jim-mullen.com), Mullens is a new entrant to Wrigleyville.

Murphy's Bleachers

3655 N. Sheffield Ave.
773-281-5356

This institution within steps of the entrance to the Wrigley Field bleachers is always packed. A few tips: enter through the back; there are port-o-potties under the El tracks just behind the bar; check out the model of Wrigley Field in the rear of the bar. They make one of the best burgers around and a sign near the bar counts down the days to the Opener.

Nisei

3439 N. Sheffield Ave.
773-525-0557

A little bit of history – 40 years ago this was one of the few places in town that residents of Japanese descent could meet (Nisei means second-generation Japanese-American). It's still a lively bar, with an extensive collection of beers at good prices.

The Outpost

3438 N. Clark St.
773-244-1166

Smart, casual and a neighborhood favorite for fresh inventive dishes accompanied by an extensive wine list. Also known for stocking an impressive array of whisky; Sunday brunch and small outdoor seating area.

Penny's Noodle Shop

3400 N. Sheffield Ave.
773-281-8222

This triangle-shaped restaurant serves great noodles, satays, and other Thai specialities at good prices. Expect a wait – but the food and the value are worth it.

The Pepper Lounge
3441 N. Sheffield Ave.
773-665-7377

Authentic bar/lounge. Tables are close, but that's part of the fun. Secret courtyard with lots of private tables during good weather. Fun and festive.

The Piano Man
3801 N. Clark St.
773-868-9611

The man who used to play the piano in the corner and for whom the bar is named is gone, but this is a sure bet for after-game drinks, with a little more room than Bernie's or Murphy's. Rub elbows with the police and firemen who enjoy this bar, and bringing in food from nearby restaurants is permitted.

Pick Me Up
3408 N. Clark St.
773-248-6613

Diner? Coffee House? Café? Whatever label you give this funky place it is hopping late at night – open 'til 3:00 a.m. most nights, and 24 hours on Saturday and Sunday. Enjoy a late night breakfast or some of the simple comfort food available. And coffee is ever present if you need it.

Pizano's
3466 N. Clark St.
773-244-1766

The Malnati family does it again – deep dish Chicago-style pizza. Their secret recipes continue to turn out pizzas with great sauces. Chocolate chip cookie and ice cream dessert may be the best part of the visit.

P.S. Bangkok
3345 N. Clark St.
773-871-7777

Take out. Eat In. Enjoy Sunday Brunch. Always a good value, plus ask if they still give a 20-percent discount with your Cubs ticket stub.

Raw Bar
3720 N. Clark St.
773-348-7291

Don't be fooled by the name – only the oysters are raw. The daiquiris are the house specialty. One room is a raucous bar. The other side is called the Ivory Lounge and features live music. The menu is filled with an ever-changing array of seafood and meat selections; the crispy salmon filet comes highly recommended.

Redmond's

3358 N. Sheffield Ave.
773-404-2151

Across from Penny's. Can be less crowded than most of the sports bars. Typical bar fare – though they do have a changing menu of wraps.

Salt & Pepper Diner

3537 N. Clark St.
773-883-9800

This 50's-style diner serves up a variety of good, cheap food all day long. They also serve beer if you want an alternative to the bar scene.

Sheffield's

3258 N. Sheffield Ave.
773-281-4989

Big outdoor patio with picnic tables and a huge selection of imported beers. If you haven't gotten to payday yet, ask for the "bad beer of the month" and you'll get a bottle for $1.50 – buyer beware.

Sluggers

3540 N. Clark St.
773-248-0055

Sports, sports and more sports. TVs all over the place, including two big screens. You drink here and also show your physical prowess with the batting cages, mini-bowling and High-Ball (Involves a trampoline and a basketball) upstairs. See story on page 48 of your Wise Guide.

Smart Bar

3730 N. Clark St.
773-549-4140

Downstairs from Metro. Changing acts and DJs – but always hopping. Check www.chicagoreader.com for what's on the schedule.

Spot 6

3343 N. Clark St.
773-388-0185

Not sure what happened to the other five spots. Don't complain to the owner about the orange walls – he loves the color. Enjoy this hip new trendy dance venue on two levels. No cover. Low-priced cocktails.

Sports Corner Grill
952 W. Addison St.
773-929-1441

At under 50 steps (depending how straight you're walking) from the SE corner of Wrigley, this place is, like, convenient. Loads of TVs, bar food and beer.

Sweet Occasions and More
3731 N. Clark St.
773-868-1940

Just like the name says, it offers a wide variety of treats and eats. Aside from the variety of ice creams, there are many different flavors of Hawaiian Kona Coffee.

Trace
3714 N. Clark St.
773-477-3400

It's all about the beer. A neighborhood hangout with a wide variety of draft and bottled beer on two levels. A nice departure. Often a DJ later in the week.

Tryst
3485 N. Clark St.
773-755-3980

One of several new spots that break the Irish sports stranglehold on Wrigleyville. Food is good, reasonably priced and goes with the requisite list of martinis.

Tuscany
3700 N. Clark St.
773-404-7700

Outpost of a Little Italy favorite; good food and wine list. Upscale for this area, so a great place to bring the in-laws after the game or to entertain a client.

Twist
3412 N. Sheffield Ave.
773-388-2727

Interesting tapas. Another good alternative to the sports-bar routine. Inventive dishes and pitchers of sangria make this a good choice.

Twisted Spoke
3369 N. Clark St.
773-525-5300

As the name might imply, this biker-themed bar and restaurant offers good food and drink, and a bit of a different scene then you might find in the rest of Wrigleyville. We recommend trying the pulled-pork sandwich.

Uncommon Ground Coffeehouse and Café

3800 N. Clark St.
773-929-3680

No need to frequent a popular coffee chain when you can sip java outdoors or in the window at Uncommon Ground. Local musicians often entertain. Great soups and pastries baked on the premises daily. Healthy organic selections.

The Wild Hare

3530 N. Clark St.
773-327-4273

Red Stripe and Rum Punch. At the Wild Hare pack in with the Jamaicans and you'll be part of the family in no time. National and international reggae groups make this a regular stop.

Wrigleyville Dogs

3737 N. Clark St.
773-296-1500

Hot dogs 24 hours a day.

Yak-Zies Bar and Grill

3710 N. Clark St.
773-525-9200

A great group spot – get energized before the game or gather afterwards. When the weather is great the windows open to the street and there is a huge patio. Lots of beers, TVs and pub fare. Buffalo Wings are some of the best in Chicago.

Useful Websites

Events
www.cityofchicago.org
www.chicagoevents.com
www.metromix.com

Restaurants

www.metromix.com
Operated by the Chicago Tribune, this site has the 411 on pretty
much every restaurant, club, bar and event in the Chicago area.

centerstage.net/neighborhoods/wrigleyville.html
Similar to www.metromix.com, this particular page focuses on
Wrigleyville.

Cubs Stuff

www.cubs.com
The official Cubs site.

www.chicagosports.com
Tribune's Chicago sports site.

www.theheckler.com
Think "The Onion" for Cubs fans. Look for a hard copy of the
newsletter around Wrigleyville for some pre-game laughs.

www.cubsbetweenthevines.com
A newsletter with information about the team.

www.ronniewoowoo.com
Official website of the famous screaming Cubs fan.

http://eamuscatuli.blogspot.com and northside.blogspot.com
If you like the blog thing.

Driving Directions and Parking

The Cubs offer driving directions on their website and advice on parking. Public transportation is the best bet, but if you must drive, there are various parking lots around Wrigley Field and residents who'll let you park behind their homes or apartments. Just drive down the surrounding residential streets -you'll see them holding up signs and waving you in. If you're headed to a day game during the week you can occasionally find street parking, as long as you're out by the time the sun goes down and parking restrictions kick in. You can't park anywhere on the street near Wrigley for night games without a residency permit. If you know someone who lives in the area they often have extras you can stick on your windshield.
www.chicago.cubs.mlb.com/NASApp/mlb/chc/ballpark/directions.jsp

Biking to Wrigley

Parking around Wrigley is brutal, the El is always packed on game day and not all of us are lucky enough to live within walking distance of the park. There is another alternative: think two wheels, think pedaling, think exercise. The Cubs recently added a free bike check located in a former car wash right next to the ballpark (just off the corner of Clark and Waveland). Hand over your bike to an attendant and they'll secure it for up to an hour after the game. Service starts two hours before first pitch.

ATMs at Wrigley Field

Outside Gate D: Three ATMs next to the ticket windows
Inside Gate D: Next to the Sheffield Grill
Inside Gate F: On the far side next to the hot dog stand
Upper Deck: On the food patio behind home plate
Bleachers: Mid-way point of the main bleacher ramp

Cubs Cash: An alternative to waiting in ATM lines, Cubs cash can be purchased with a credit card (no markups/fees) at the ticket windows inside the park near Gate F. Accepted just like cash in the ballpark, you'll get cash as change.

City of Chicago Events

7th Annual Mayor Daley's Kids and Kites Festival
May 14 & October 1

7th Annual Great Chicago Places and Spaces
May 20-22

21st Annual Chicago Gospel Music Festival
Millennium Park
June 3-5

Belmont-Sheffield Music Festival
N. Sheffield-Belmont to School
June 4-5 (Noon to 10pm)

22nd Annual Chicago Blues Festival
Grant Park
June 9-12

Lincoln Park Fest
Clark & Armitage
June 18-19 (11am to 8pm)

25th Annual Taste of Chicago
Grant Park
June 24-July 4

Pride Fest
Halsted & Waveland
June 25 (Noon to 9pm)

15th Annual Chicago Country Music Festival
Grant Park
June 25-26

Lakeview Arts & Music Festival
Belmont, N. Lincoln & Ashland
July 2-3 (Noon to 10pm)

8th Annual Chicago Folk & Roots Festival Welles Park
Lincoln & Montrose
July 9-10 (Noon – 9:30pm)

Wrigleyville's Addison-Clark Street Fair
Clark & Addison
July 9-10 (Noon to 10:30pm)

6th Annual Chicago Outdoor Film Festival
Butler Field, Grant Park
July 12-Aug 23 (Tuesdays at dusk)

48th Annual Venetian Night
Lakefront between Shedd and Monroe Harbor
July 30 (8:30pm)

Taste of Lincoln Avenue
N. Lincoln between Fullerton &
Wrightwood
July 30-31 (Noon to 10pm)

Northalsted Market Days
N. Halsted between Belmont
& Addison
August 6-7 (11am to 10pm)

**47th Annual Chicago Air
and Water Show**
Lakefront
August 20-21

**17th Annual Viva! Chicago
Latin Music Festival**
Grant Park
August 27-28

**27th Annual Chicago Jazz
Festival**
Grant Park
September 1-4

**9th Annual Celtic Fest
Chicago**
Grant Park
September 17-18

Oktoberfest
Belle Plaine between Lincoln
& Damen
September 23-25
*Fri: 5-10pm, Sat: 3-10:30pm,
Sun: 11am-7pm*

*Check out www.cityofchicago.org or www.chicagoevents.com
for more information*

Wrigley Field Ground Rules

Unlike any other pro sport, baseball rules differ depending on the stadium. Below are the ground rules for Wrigley Field (from www.cubs.com).

Baseball hits top or face of screen in front of bleacher wall and bounces back on playing field **(In Play)**

Baseball hits top of screen and drops between screen and wall **(Home Run)**

Baseball hits screen and bounces into bleachers **(Home Run)**

Baseball sticks in screen in front of bleachers **(Double)**

Baseball sticks in vines on bleacher wall **(Double)**

Baseball comes out of vines **(In Play)**

Baseball hits left field or right field foul markers above painted mark **(Home Run)**

Baseball hits foul markers below painted mark and bounces back on playing field **(In Play)**

Baseball goes under grates in left field or right field and remains there **(Double)**

Baseball goes in or under grates on either side of home plate and remains there **(Pitched Ball: One Base, Thrown Ball: Two Bases)**

Also: *Players cannot enter the dugout steps at Wrigley Field to catch any foul pop fly.*

Vicinity Map

Use these reference points to find your way around Wrigleyville.

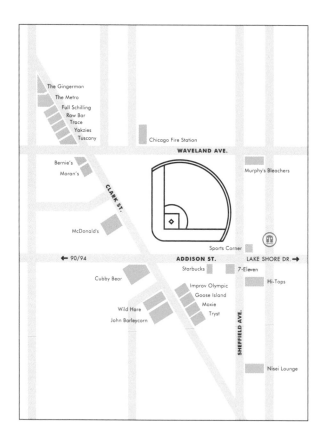

2005 Complete Schedule

(All times Central; source is www.cubs.com)

April

Monday, April 4	@ Diamondbacks	4:10 PM	WGN	WGN 720
Tuesday, April 5	@ Diamondbacks	8:40 PM	CSN+	WGN 720
Wednesday, April 6	@ Diamondbacks	8:40 PM	CSN Chicago	WGN 720
Friday, April 8	vs Brewers	1:20 PM	WGN	WGN 720
Saturday, April 9	vs Brewers	1:20 PM	CSN Chicago	WGN 720
Sunday, April 10	vs Brewers	1:20 PM	WGN	WGN 720
Monday, April 11	vs Padres	1:20 PM	WGN	WGN 720
Tuesday, April 12	vs Padres	1:20 PM	CSN Chicago	WGN 720
Wednesday, April 13	vs Padres	1:20 PM	WGN	WGN 720
Friday, April 15	@ Pirates	6:05 PM	CSN+	WGN 720
Saturday, April 16	@ Pirates	6:05 PM	CSN Chicago	WGN 720
Sunday, April 17	@ Pirates	12:35 PM	WGN	WGN 720
Monday, April 18	@ Reds	6:10 PM	CSN Chicago	WGN 720
Tuesday, April 19	@ Reds	6:10 PM	WCIU	WGN 720
Wednesday, April 20	@ Cardinals	6:10 PM	CSN Chicago	WGN 720
Thursday, April 21	@ Cardinals	12:10 PM	CSN Chicago	WGN 720
Friday, April 22	vs Pirates	2:20 PM	WGN	WGN 720
Saturday, April 23	vs Pirates	1:20 PM	CSN Chicago	WGN 720
Sunday, April 24	vs Pirates	1:20 PM	WGN	WGN 720
Monday, April 25	vs Reds	7:05 PM	WCIU	WGN 720
Tuesday, April 26	vs Reds	7:05 PM	CSN Chicago	WGN 720
Wednesday, April 27	vs Reds	1:20 PM	WGN	WGN 720
Friday, April 29	@ Astros	7:05 PM	WGN	WGN 720
Saturday, April 30	@ Astros	6:05 PM	CSN Chicago	WGN 720

May

Sunday, May 1	@ Astros	1:05 PM	WGN	WGN 720
Tuesday, May 3	@ Brewers	7:05 PM	CSN Chicago	WGN 720
Wednesday, May 4	@ Brewers	7:05 PM	CSN+	WGN 720
Thursday, May 5	@ Brewers	12:05 PM	WGN	WGN 720
Friday, May 6	vs Phillies	2:20 PM	WGN	WGN 720

Saturday, May 7	vs Phillies	1:20 PM	CSN Chicago	WGN 720
Sunday, May 8	vs Phillies	1:20 PM	WGN	WGN 720
Monday, May 9	vs Mets	7:05 PM	WCIU	WGN 720
Tuesday, May 10	vs Mets	7:05 PM	CSN Chicago	WGN 720
Wednesday, May 11	vs Mets	1:20 PM	WGN	WGN 720
Friday, May 13	@ Nationals	6:05 PM	CSN+	WGN 720
Saturday, May 14	@ Nationals	6:05 PM	CSN Chicago	WGN 720
Sunday, May 15	@ Nationals	12:05 PM	WGN	WGN 720
Tuesday, May 17	@ Pirates	6:05 PM	WCIU	WGN 720
Wednesday, May 18	@ Pirates	11:35 AM	CSN Chicago	WGN 720
Friday, May 20	vs White Sox	1:20 PM	CSN Chicago	WGN 720
Saturday, May 21	vs White Sox	12:20 PM	FOX	WGN 720
Sunday, May 22	vs White Sox	1:20 PM	WGN	WGN 720
Monday, May 23	vs Astros	7:05 PM	CSN Chicago	WGN 720
Tuesday, May 24	vs Astros	7:05 PM	WGN	WGN 720
Wednesday, May 25	vs Astros	6:05 PM	CSN Chicago	WGN 720
Thursday, May 26	vs Rockies	1:20 PM	WGN	WGN 720
Friday, May 27	vs Rockies	1:20 PM	CSN Chicago	WGN 720
Saturday, May 28	vs Rockies	12:05 PM	CSN Chicago	WGN 720
Sunday, May 29	vs Rockies	1:20 PM	CSN Chicago	WGN 720
Monday, May 30	@ Dodgers	7:10 PM	CSN Chicago	WGN 720
Tuesday, May 31	@ Dodgers	9:10 PM	WGN	WGN 720

June

Wednesday, June 1	@ Dodgers	9:10 PM	CSN+	WGN 720
Thursday, June 2	@ Padres	9:05 PM	WGN	WGN 720
Friday, June 3	@ Padres	9:05 PM	CSN Chicago	WGN 720
Saturday, June 4	@ Padres	9:05 PM	WGN	WGN 720
Sunday, June 5	@ Padres	3:05 PM	CSN Chicago	WGN 720
Monday, June 6	vs Blue Jays	7:05 PM	WGN	WGN 720
Tuesday, June 7	vs Blue Jays	7:05 PM	CSN Chicago	WGN 720
Wednesday, June 8	vs Blue Jays	1:20 PM	WGN	WGN 720
Friday, June 10	vs Red Sox	1:20 PM	WGN	WGN 720
Saturday, June 11	vs Red Sox	2:15 PM	FOX	WGN 720
Sunday, June 12	vs Red Sox	7:05 PM	ESPN	WGN 720
Monday, June 13	vs Marlins	7:05 PM	CSN Chicago	WGN 720
Tuesday, June 14	vs Marlins	7:05 PM	WGN	WGN 720

Appendix

Wednesday, June 15	vs Marlins	1:20 PM	WGN	WGN 720
Friday, June 17	@ Yankees	6:05 PM	WGN	WGN 720
Saturday, June 18	@ Yankees	2:15 PM	FOX	WGN 720
Sunday, June 19	@ Yankees	12:05 PM	CSN Chicago	WGN 720
Monday, June 20	@ Brewers	7:05 PM	CSN Chicago	WGN 720
Tuesday, June 21	@ Brewers	7:05 PM	WGN	WGN 720
Wednesday, June 22	@ Brewers	7:05 PM	CSN Chicago	WGN 720
Thursday, June 23	@ Brewers	1:05 PM	WGN	WGN 720
Friday, June 24	@ White Sox	3:05 PM	CSN Chicago, WGN	WGN 720
Saturday, June 25	@ White Sox	3:05 PM	WGN	WGN 720
Sunday, June 26	@ White Sox	2:05 PM	CSN Chicago, WGN	WGN 720
Tuesday, June 28	vs Brewers	7:05 PM	CSN Chicago	WGN 720
Wednesday, June 29	vs Brewers	1:20 PM	CSN Chicago	WGN 720
Thursday, June 30	vs Brewers	1:20 PM	WGN	WGN 720

July

Friday, July 1	vs Nationals	1:20 PM	CSN Chicago	WGN 720
Saturday, July 2	vs Nationals	3:05 PM	WGN	WGN 720
Sunday, July 3	vs Nationals	1:20 PM	WGN	WGN 720
Monday, July 4	@ Braves	6:05 PM	WGN	WGN 720
Tuesday, July 5	@ Braves	6:35 PM	CSN Chicago	WGN 720
Wednesday, July 6	@ Braves	6:05 PM	CSN Chicago	WGN 720
Thursday, July 7	@ Braves	6:35 PM	WGN	WGN 720
Friday, July 8	@ Marlins	6:35 PM	CSN+	WGN 720
Saturday, July 9	@ Marlins	5:05 PM	CSN Chicago	WGN 720
Sunday, July 10	@ Marlins	12:05 PM	WGN	WGN 720
Friday, July 15	vs Pirates	1:20 PM	CSN Chicago	WGN 720
Saturday, July 16	vs Pirates	3:05 PM	WGN	WGN 720
Sunday, July 17	vs Pirates	1:20 PM	WGN	WGN 720
Monday, July 18	@ Reds	6:10 PM	CSN Chicago	WGN 720
Tuesday, July 19	@ Reds	6:10 PM	WGN	WGN 720
Wednesday, July 20	@ Reds	6:10 PM	CSN Chicago	WGN 720
Thursday, July 21	@ Reds	11:35 AM	CSN Chicago	WGN 720
Friday, July 22	@ Cardinals	7:10 PM	WGN	WGN 720
Saturday, July 23	@ Cardinals	2:15 PM	FOX	WGN 720
Sunday, July 24	@ Cardinals	1:15 PM		WGN 720
Monday, July 25	vs Giants	7:05 PM	CSN Chicago	WGN 720

Tuesday, July 26	vs Giants	7:05 PM	WGN	WGN 720
Wednesday, July 27	vs Giants	1:20 PM	WGN	WGN 720
Thursday, July 28	vs Diamondbacks	1:20 PM	CSN Chicago	WGN 720
Friday, July 29	vs Diamondbacks	1:20 PM	WGN	WGN 720
Saturday, July 30	vs Diamondbacks	3:05 PM	WGN	WGN 720
Sunday, July 31	vs Diamondbacks	1:20 PM	WGN	WGN 720

August

Tuesday, August 2	@ Phillies	6:05 PM	CSN Chicago	WGN 720
Wednesday, August 3	@ Phillies	6:05 PM	CSN+	WGN 720
Thursday, August 4	@ Phillies	12:05 PM	WGN	WGN 720
Friday, August 5	@ Mets	6:10 PM	WGN	WGN 720
Saturday, August 6	@ Mets	12:20 PM	FOX	WGN 720
Sunday, August 7	@ Mets	12:10 PM		WGN 720
Monday, August 8	vs Reds	7:05 PM	WGN	WGN 720
Tuesday, August 9	vs Reds	1:20 PM	WGN	WGN 720
Wednesday, August 10	vs Reds	1:20 PM	CSN Chicago	WGN 720
Thursday, August 11	vs Cardinals	1:20 PM	CSN Chicago	WGN 720
Friday, August 12	vs Cardinals	1:20 PM	WGN	WGN 720
Saturday, August 13	vs Cardinals	12:20 PM	FOX	WGN 720
Sunday, August 14	vs Cardinals	TBD		WGN 720
Monday, August 15	@ Astros	7:05 PM	CSN Chicago	WGN 720
Tuesday, August 16	@ Astros	7:05 PM	WGN	WGN 720
Wednesday, August 17	@ Astros	7:05 PM	CSN Chicago	WGN 720
Friday, August 19	@ Rockies	4:05 PM	CSN Chicago	WGN 720
Saturday, August 20	@ Rockies	7:05 PM	WGN	WGN 720
Sunday, August 21	@ Rockies	2:05 PM	WGN	WGN 720
Monday, August 22	vs Braves	7:05 PM	CSN Chicago	WGN 720
Tuesday, August 23	vs Braves	7:05 PM	CSN Chicago	WGN 720
Wednesday, August 24	vs Braves	1:20 PM	WGN	WGN 720
Friday, August 26	vs Marlins	1:20 PM	WGN	WGN 720
Saturday, August 27	vs Marlins	3:05 PM	CSN Chicago	WGN 720
Sunday, August 28	vs Marlins	1:20 PM	WGN	WGN 720
Monday, August 29	vs Dodgers	7:05 PM	CSN Chicago	WGN 720
Tuesday, August 30	vs Dodgers	7:05 PM	WGN	WGN 720
Wednesday, August 31	vs Dodgers	1:20 PM	WGN	WGN 720

September

Friday, September 2	@ Pirates	6:05 PM	CSN+	WGN 720
Saturday, September 3	@ Pirates	11:35 AM	CSN Chicago	WGN 720
Sunday, September 4	@ Pirates	12:35 PM	WGN	WGN 720
Monday, September 5	@ Cardinals	1:15 PM	WGN	WGN 720
Tuesday, September 6	@ Cardinals	7:10 PM	WGN	WGN 720
Wednesday, September 7	@ Cardinals	7:10 PM	CSN Chicago	WGN 720
Thursday, September 8	@ Giants	9:15 PM	WGN	WGN 720
Friday, September 9	@ Giants	9:15 PM	CSN Chicago	WGN 720
Saturday, September 10	@ Giants	3:05 PM		WGN 720
Sunday, September 11	@ Giants	3:05 PM	WGN	WGN 720
Monday, September 12	vs Reds	7:05 PM	CSN Chicago	WGN 720
Tuesday, September 13	vs Reds	7:05 PM	WCIU	WGN 720
Wednesday, September 14	vs Reds	7:05 PM	CSN Chicago	WGN 720
Thursday, September 15	vs Cardinals	7:05 PM	WGN	WGN 720
Friday, September 16	vs Cardinals	2:20 PM	CSN Chicago	WGN 720
Saturday, September 17	vs Cardinals	12:20 PM	FOX	WGN 720
Sunday, September 18	vs Cardinals	1:20 PM	WGN	WGN 720
Tuesday, September 20	@ Brewers	6:35 PM	WCIU	WGN 720
Wednesday, September 21	@ Brewers	6:35 PM	CSN+	WGN 720
Thursday, September 22	@ Brewers	1:05 PM	CSN Chicago	WGN 720
Friday, September 23	vs Astros	2:20 PM	WGN	WGN 720
Saturday, September 24	vs Astros	1:20 PM	CSN Chicago	WGN 720
Sunday, September 25	vs Astros	1:20 PM	WGN	WGN 720
Tuesday, September 27	vs Pirates	7:05 PM	WCIU	WGN 720
Wednesday, September 28	vs Pirates	1:20 PM	WGN	WGN 720
Thursday, September 29	@ Astros	7:05 PM	CSN Chicago	WGN 720
Friday, September 30	@ Astros	7:05 PM	WCIU	WGN 720

October

Saturday, October 1	@ Astros	6:05 PM	CSN Chicago	WGN 720
Sunday, October 2	@ Astros	1:05 PM	WGN	WGN 720

Collect Signatures

Get your favorite players to sign here.

Autographs

Autographs

Autographs

"Baseball, it is said, is only a game. True. And the Grand Canyon is only a hole in Arizona."

  – George F. Will in *Men at Work: The Craft of Baseball*

The bulk of this book comes from the personal experiences and observations of the authors, who have spent many years taking in games at Wrigley Field and sampling much of what the neighborhood and city have to offer. For some of the finer points – historical dates, addresses and phone numbers – we consulted the Chicago Cubs media guide, the team website www.cubs.com and other MLB official sites, the City of Chicago website www.cityofchicago.org and www.metromix.com.

We hope you find this book informative, occasionally funny, and the perfect compliment to a day at Wrigley Field.